WRITERS

General Editor: Simon Trussler

Associate Editor: Malcolm Page

BOND
on File

Compiled by Philip Roberts

Ex Libris
Arthur E. and
Nora A. McGuinness

Methuen. London and New York

First published in 1985 in
simultaneous hardback and paperback editions
by Methuen London Ltd,
11 New Fetter Lane, London EC4P 4EE
and Methuen Inc, 733 Third Avenue,
New York, NY 10017

Copyright in the compilation
© 1985 by Philip Roberts
Copyright in the series format
© 1985 by Methuen London Ltd
Copyright in the editorial presentation
© 1985 by Simon Trussler

Typeset in IBM 9pt Press Roman
by 🡒 Tek-Art, Croydon, Surrey
Printed in Great Britain by
Hazell Watson & Viney Ltd
Member of the BPCC Group
Aylesbury, Bucks

British Library Cataloguing in Publication Data

Roberts, Philip, 1942-
    Bond on file. — (Writers on file)
    1. Bond, Edward — Criticism and interpretation
    I. Title   II. Series
    822'.914   PR6052.05Z

ISBN 0 413 58520 4 (Hardback)
       0 413 54040 5 (Paperback)

Cover image based on a photo by Chris Davies

This book is published in both hardback
and paperback editions. The paperback edition
is sold subject to the condition that it
shall not, by way of trade or otherwise,
be lent, resold, hired out, or otherwise
circulated without the publisher's prior consent
in any form of binding or cover other than
that in which it is published and without
a similar condition including this condition
being imposed on the subsequent purchaser.

Contents

Acknowledgements

My thanks are due to Edward Bond, who allowed me access to his private notebooks and correspondence, and was kind enough to read the typescript; to Elisabeth Bond, who supplied useful information; to Margaret Ramsay who, as Edward Bond's agent, permitted me to study her files; and to Mrs. Vera Dyer, whose typing is impeccable. I am obliged to the University of Sheffield, which granted me leave of absence in order to complete this work, and to the University Research Fund, which aided part of its preparation.

The theatre is, by its nature, an ephemeral art: yet it is a daunting task to track down the newspaper reviews, or contemporary statements from the writer or his director, which are often all that remain to help us recreate some sense of what a particular production was like. This series is therefore intended to make readily available a selection of the comments that the critics made about the plays of leading modern dramatists at the time of their production − and to trace, too, the course of each writer's own views about his work and his world.

In addition to combining a uniquely convenient source of such elusive *documentation,* the 'Writers on File' series also assembles the *information* necessary for readers to pursue further their interest in a particular writer or work. Variations in quantity between one writer's output and another, differences in temperament which make some readier than others to talk about their work, and the variety of critical response, all mean that the presentation and balance of material shifts between one volume and another: but we have tried to arrive at a format for the series which will nevertheless enable users of one volume readily to find their way around any other.

Section 1, 'A Brief Chronology', provides a quick conspective overview of each playwright's life and career. *Section 2* deals with the plays themselves, arranged chronologically in the order of their composition: information on first performances, major revivals, and publication is followed by a brief synopsis (for quick reference set in slightly larger, italic type), then by a representative selection of the critical response, and of the dramatist's own comments on the play and its theme.

Section 3 offers concise guidance to each writer's work in non-dramatic forms, while *Section 4,* 'The Writer on His Work', brings together comments from the playwright himself on more general matters of construction, opinion, and artistic development. Finally, *Section 5* provides a bibliographical guide to other primary and secondary sources of further reading, among which full details will be found of works cited elsewhere under short titles, and of collected editions of the plays − but not of individual titles, particulars of which will be found with the other factual data in Section 2.

The 'Writers on File' series hopes by striking this kind

General Editor's Introduction

of balance between information and a wide range of opinion to offer 'companions' to the study of major playwrights in the modern repertoire — not in that dangerous pre-digested fashion which can too readily quench the desire to read the plays themselves , nor so prescriptively as to allow any single line of approach to predominate, but rather to encourage readers to form their own judgements of the plays, to set against the many views here represented.

Among British dramatists of the present century, Edward Bond is probably second only to Bernard Shaw in having consistently explicated the concerns of his plays not only in prefaces to the texts, but in poems, short stories, and other related pieces, such as *The Activists Papers.* Since these are readily available alongside the scripts, preference here has been given to including those utterances of Bond's which reveal something of the development of his thinking, and the background to his craft.

Such extracts are set illuminatingly alongside the critical judgements which have vilified and with no less passion defended Bond's work since *Saved* first burst upon its audiences. Interestingly, the actors quoted in this volume remark on how different is the *quality* of an audience's response to Bond, and one suspects that this derives from his ability, unique in the British theatre, to tap the very wellsprings of human feeling while preserving a sort of epic detachment of style. Hence, perhaps, the frequent, literal-minded confusion between 'what happens' on stage and what a play is *about.*

Bond's personal standpoint has developed from a humane but almost helpless sympathy for the view of life he presents, to a dialectically assured feeling (no less offensive to some in its very assurance) for the possibility of change. In spite of a capacity for touches of comedy both high and low, he is fundamentally a serious writer, unwilling to supply the sort of sugar-coating craved by many British audiences: thus, there has often been a warmer response to his work abroad, in countries with a readier acceptance of the theatre as an appropriate place for such seriousness. This little volume illuminates the work of one of today's most important writers for the theatre.

Simon Trussler

1934   18 July, born in Holloway, North London, one of four children: 'Lower working class. But not London working class – my parents had come up to London during the depression because they couldn't get work on the land. My father had been a labourer in [East Anglia] and he did various kinds of labouring jobs when he was in London'.

1940   Evacuated to Cornwall and subsequently to his grandparents near Ely.

1944   Returned to London and attended Crouch End Secondary Modern School. Not allowed to take the eleven-plus exam. Left when fifteen: 'That was the making of me, of course. You see, after that nobody takes you seriously. The conditioning process stops. Once you let them send you to grammar school and university, you're ruined'.

1948   Saw Wolfit's *Macbeth* at the Bedford Theatre, Camden Town – 'the first thing that made sense of my life for me. . . . Naturally, when I wrote, I wrote for the theatre'. During his childhood, watched music hall performances, where his sister worked: 'It's the most incredible way to develop an understanding of timing and control on a stage. . . . A wonderful way to learn about the theatre'.

1953   Began two years National Service, and wrote his first serious work, a short story, while stationed in Vienna: 'I was in the infantry, cut off from the outside world for six weeks – degrading, hair cut, strange clothes, shouted at, screamed at. We were turned into automata'.

1958   Submitted two plays, *Klaxon in Atreus' Place* and *The Fiery Tree*, to the recently established English Stage Company at the Royal Court Theatre, London. Invited to join their Writers' Group, and became a regular play reader for the theatre: 'In this group we practised improvisation and a few elementary acting exercises. The group was always run by directors and not writers. This was good because it made the members aware of the plastic, visual nature of theatre'.

1962   9 Dec., his first performed play, *The Pope's Wedding*, given a single 'production without decor' at

the Royal Court, whose Artistic Director, George Devine, com-
missioned a new play as a result.

1964   18 Sept., *Saved* submitted to the Royal Court.

1965   William Gaskill, Devine's successor, decided to present
Saved privately for members of the English Stage Society, after
the Lord Chamberlain's office had returned the play together
with a demand for cuts in the text. Bond became a full-time
writer as *Saved* began rehearsing. 3 Nov., first performance,
disturbed by demonstrations in the theatre. 18 Dec., police
officers visited the theatre. Bond a finalist for the award of
'Most Promising Playwright' of 1965.

1966   Jan., the Royal Court charged under the Theatres Act of
1843 with presenting an unlicensed play *(Saved)*. 13 Jan., Bond's
adaptation of Middleton's *A Chaste Maid in Cheapside* given at
the Royal Court. 3 Feb., Bond offered an Arts Council bursary of
£1000. 14 Feb., court proceedings opened. 17 Feb., theatre
censorship debated in the House of Lords. 1 April, Royal Court
found guilty; defendants given conditional discharge. Nov.,
Bond bought a house outside Cambridge: 'my house is on the
edge of Wilbraham, and I'm known here as "the last man in
the village".'

1967   18 Apr., Bond's version of *Three Sisters* opened at the
Royal Court. 8 Nov., *Early Morning* banned in its entirety by the
Lord Chamberlain: returned without comment except that 'His
Lordship would not allow it'. 9 Nov., plans made to present the
play for members of the English Stage Society. The Arts Council
threatened the Royal Court with loss of grant if it went ahead.
Saved, directed by Peter Stein in Munich, voted best play and
production of 1967 by *Theater Heute. Saved* also premiered in
Austria, Argentina, Norway, and Sweden.

1968   31 Mar., the Sunday-night production of *Early Morning*
at the Royal Court 'celebrates the twelfth anniversary of the
English Stage Company'. Police questioned the theatre's licensee
and Artistic Director. 7 Apr., evening performance cancelled, and
a private dress rehearsal for critics performed during the afternoon. May, Bond given the George Devine Award for *Saved* and
Early Morning. 24 June, *Narrow Road to the Deep North* opened
at the Belgrade, Coventry, after demands for cuts by the Lord
Chamberlain. 28 Sept., the Theatres Bill, removing control of
plays from the Lord Chamberlain, became law. Bond given the
John Whiting Award for *Narrow Road. Saved* given fourteen
productions in West Germany and premiered in Holland, Den-

mark, Japan, Czechoslovakia, and USA.

1969 Edward Bond season at the Royal Court: 7 Feb., *Saved* (first public performance); 19 Feb., *Narrow Road;* 13 Mar., *Early Morning* (first public performance). Apr., Bond contributed to *The Enoch Show* at the Royal Court, the first performance of which was disrupted by members of the National Front, 15 Sept.-3 Oct., tour of *Saved* and *Narrow Road* to Belgrade, Venice, Prague, Lublin, and Warsaw. *Saved* awarded a prize at the BITEF Festival, Belgrade. Nov., *Narrow Road* given as the inaugural production at the Théâtre de Nice, despite local objections.

1970 22 Mar., *Black Mass* performed for the Anti-Apartheid movement at the Lyceum Theatre, with Bond playing Christ.

1971 11 Apr., *Passion* performed for CND rally at Alexandra Park racecourse. 29 Sept., *Lear* given at the Royal Court.

1972 17 June, spoke at the 'China and Britain' forum, Roundhouse, London.

1973 27 Jan., *Lear,* directed by Bond, opened in Vienna. 22 May, *The Sea* first performed at the Royal Court. Oct., the Berlin Schillertheater's *Lear* won a prize at the Belgrade Festival. 14 Nov., *Bingo* premiered at the Northcott Theatre, Exeter.

1974 28 May, Bond's translation of Wedekind's *Spring Awakening* performed at the National Theatre. 10 Nov., contributed to 'Poets to the People' at the Mermaid Theatre for the Defence Aid Fund of Southern Africa.

1975 Oct., Bond a founder member of the Theatre Writers' Group (now the Theatre Writers' Union). 18 Nov., *The Fool* premiered at the Royal Court.

1976 27 May, Yale Repertory Theatre's *Bingo* awarded a Special Citation in the 21st Obie Awards. 8 June, *Stone* performed by Gay Sweatshop at the Institute of Contemporary Arts, London. 12 July, *We Come to the River* premiered at Covent Garden, and on the same evening Bond's adaptation of Webster's *The White Devil* first performed at the Old Vic Theatre. 25 Oct., *Grandma Faust* (the first play of *A-A-America!)* performed at the Almost Free Theatre. 22 Nov., *The Swing* (the second play of *A-A-America!)* given at the same theatre. *The Fool* voted Best Play of 1976 by *Plays and Players.*

1977 May, accepted an Honorary Doctorate, Yale University. Oct., took up a two-year Northern Arts Literary Fellowship in the Universities of Newcastle and Durham.

1978   13 Jan., *The Bundle* premiered at the Warehouse Theatre, London. 10 Aug., *The Woman* becomes the first new play to be staged in the Olivier auditorium of the National Theatre. *Theatre Poems and Songs* published.

1979   8 Mar., *The Worlds*, directed by Bond, opened at the Newcastle Playhouse. 17 Mar., *Orpheus: a Story in Six Scenes*, performed by the Stuttgart Ballet.

1980   Feb., London Weekend Television's *South Bank Show* devoted to Bond's work. *The Activists Papers* published, together with *The Worlds*. 3 Nov., prominent in the defence of Howard Brenton's *The Romans in Britain*, privately prosecuted for obscenity, with an article published in *The Guardian*.

1981   22 July, *Restoration* first performed at the Royal Court.

1982   27 Jan., *Summer* opened at the National Theatre. *Derek* performed at the Youth Festival, Royal Shakespeare Theatre, Stratford, in Oct. Some of Bond's songs and poems, with music by David Shaw-Parker, performed at the same time in Stratford. 23 Dec., *Summer* performed on BBC Radio 3 by the original cast. A new play, *Human Cannon*, completed. Oct.-Mar. 1983, Resident Theatre Writer, University of Essex.

1983   1 Mar., *After the Assassinations* given a student production at the University of Essex. 2 June, *The Cat* given first performance at Schwetzingen, West Germany. Oct.-Nov., Visiting Professor, University of Palermo.

1984   19 Jan., *Red, Black and Ignorant* performed as part of the 'Thoughtcrimes' fortnight, Barbican Centre. 25 Jan., gave a workshop on his recent plays. 4 May, *The Tin Can People* performed by Bread and Circuses Theatre Company, Birmingham.

The order of the plays within each sub-section — Stage Plays, Music Theatre, and Translations and Adaptations — is chronological by the date of writing, an order which is not invariably reflected in the date of production (for example, *The Woman* was written before *The Bundle,* but performed later). Space precludes more than a selective list of revivals, fuller details of which to the end of 1976 may be found in *Edward Bond: a Companion to the Plays,* by Malcolm Hay and Philip Roberts (London: TQ Publications, 1978), cited below by the short title *Companion.* The short title Hay and Roberts below signifies *Bond: a Study of his Plays,* by Malcolm Hay and Philip Roberts (London: Methuen, 1980). Full particulars of all other sources cited below may be found in Section 5: A Select Bibliography.

Early Works

The following were written mainly between 1957 and 1961, and are not available for performance. Some account of them may be found in Hay and Roberts, as above.

The Tragedy, radio play.
A Woman Weeping.
The Asses of Kish (submitted for *The Observer* play competition, 1956-57).
Too Late Now, radio play (returned Dec. 1957).
Sylo's New Ruins, radio play (returned Feb. 1958).
The Performance, radio play (returned June 1958).
The Best Laid Schemes, radio play (returned Sept. 1958).
The Roller Coaster.
The Broken Shepherdess, television play.
Klaxon in Atreus' Place (submitted to the Royal Court Th., 1958).
The Fiery Tree (submitted to the Royal Court Th., 1958).
I Don't Want to be Nice, sketch for *Stars in Our Eyes* (written for the Royal Court Writers' Group, 1959).
The Golden Age (written for the Royal Court Writers' Group, Oct. 1959).
The Outing (written for the Royal Court Writers' Group, Dec. 1959 - Mar. 1960).
Kissing the Beast, television play (1960).

Later Unpublished or Unperformed Work

Sketch for *The Enoch Show*. *Performed:* Royal Court Th. Upstairs, 24 Apr. 1969.

Heads (translation and adaptation of Brecht's *Roundheads and Peakheads,* with Keith Hack). *Written:* early 1970. *Rehearsed reading:* Tyneside Th. Company, Dec. 1976.

The Master Builder (adaptation of Ibsen's play for American television). *Written:* late 1974-early 1975. *Unperformed.*

The Palace of Varieties in the Sand. Written: Dec. 1975-Jan 1976. *Unperformed.*

Text for a Ballet: for Dancers, Chorus and Orchestra. Written: Jan.-Feb. 1977. *Unperformed.*

After the Assassinations. Performed: student production, University of Essex, 1 May 1983. 'Choruses from *After the Assassinations'* published with *Derek* (London: Methuen, 1983).

The Pope's Wedding

a: Stage Plays

Play in sixteen scenes.

Written: Jan. 1961 - early 1962.

First London production: Royal Court Th., 9 Dec. 1962 (dir. Keith Johnstone).

Revived: Northcott Th., Exeter, 13 June 1973 (dir. John Dove, des. Hayden Griffin); trans. to Bush Th., 3 July 1973.

Published: London: Methuen, 1971; in *Plays and Players,* Apr. 1969; and in *Plays: One* (incorporating author's revisions).

The characters are young people drifting outside the middle-class middle ground between school and 'a career'. They come from, and speak in the idiom of, a specific local community, in this case, East Anglia. . . . There is little for any of them to relate to except each other, and the games they play to do this are generally not far from violence. . . . The most interesting character is not a member of the 'gang'. He is a 75-year-old recluse, living in a remote run-down shack amidst a daily mounting clutter of newspapers and empty tins. Alen is . . .

looked after by Pat, who promised her mother on her deathbed that she would 'doo' for him. Scopey, the most dominant person- ality in the 'gang' has married Pat and they live in a dingy, cramped flat. For Scopey, Alen is a doubly fascinating character. For one thing he lives in a place of his own on his own terms, and for another he doesn't have to go through the monotonous motions of earning his living. He gets so wrapped up in Alen's isolation that he takes over from Pat . . . and even loses his job because he spends so much time at Alen's place. Why Scopey suddenly kills Alen is not exactly clear. . . . Perhaps the only way Scopey can get any independence of the world is by robbing another man of life.

Anthony Vivis, *Flourish* (RSC newspaper), Summer 1971

The play was given one performance as a Sunday-night production without decor. Plays in this series were rehearsed to dress-rehearsal standard and shown with minimal set and costume, on a very low budget. The set for *The Pope's Wedding* was built from the set of George Devine's production of Beckett's *Happy Days.* Winnie's mound was 'turned upside down in some way, and a door was cut into it. It made a funny sort of cone shape'.

Hay and Roberts, p. 24

Congratulations on the new play, which I have at last read. Although I think it is not right yet, I do think you have made a considerable advance. The group of young people is very alive. I think the progression of the play needs more clarification. At one reading anyway it is difficult to see how the play develops dramatically from scene to scene, and although some of this could emerge during production, I think it should be clearer in the script. This refers particularly to the first half of the play.

George Devine, letter to Edward Bond, 17 Apr. 1962, quoted in Hay and Roberts, p. 23

. . . that was a series of plays to begin with [which started] with *The Pope's Wedding* and ended with *The Sea.* I had an idea about all of them before I started to write . . . that I would begin with a tragedy in which the old man would not talk. This boy Scopey keeps saying: 'Why do this?' And the old man can never say anything. He just drools. Scopey never gets an answer from him.

Bond, interviewed in *Performing Arts Journal,* I, 2 (Fall 1976)

13

The pope's wedding is an impossible ceremony — Scopey's asking for an invitation for something that isn't going to happen, that *can't* happen. ... The important thing is not to be intrigued or puzzled by images, but always to understand them. So what I wanted to do was to try and get inside the image, and see what it was all about. This is what Scopey does in the play, and in the end he kills a man and wears his clothes in order to find out. And of course there's nothing there.

Bond, interviewed in *Theatre Quarterly,* No. 5 (1972)

This bizarre and unclassifiable piece is an astonishing *tour de force* for a first play, and if it comes to that, would be an astonishing *tour de force* if it were a fifty-first. ... Mr. Bond is an original. We shall hear more of him.

Bernard Levin, *Daily Mail,* 10 Dec. 1962

Saved

Play in thirteen scenes.
Written: Mar.-Sept.1964.
First London production: Royal Court Th., 3 Nov. 1965
 (dir. William Gaskill; des. John Gunter; with John Castle as
 Len, Tony Selby as Fred, Barbara Ferris as Pam, and Gwen
 Nelson as Mary).
First American production: Yale Repertory Th., 5 Dec. 1968
 (dir. Jeff Bleckner).
Revived: Kammerspiele, Munich, 15 Apr. 1967 (dir. Peter Stein);
 Freie Volksbühne, 25 May 1968 (dir. Peter Zadek); Royal
 Court Th., 7 Feb. 1969 (dir. William Gaskill); Courtyard
 Playhouse, New York, 1 Oct. 1976 (dir. Marvin Kahan) —
 in all, more than 80 productions between 1965 and 1976.
Film version: by Star Street Film Productions for Channel 4
 television: script drafted by Bond late 1983.
Published: London: Methuen, 1966 (with 'Author's Note'),
 second ed. 1969; in *Plays and Players,* Jan. 1966; and in
 Plays: One (with a new note to *Saved,* 'On Violence').

Saved is a play about poverty in Britain now. ... Mr. Bond lays it as an actual deprivation at society's door, in all its stultifying and tragic consequences. To him, it means Pam picking up Len, taking him home to the parlour couch, scornfully amused at his horror when her father looks in. It's her jilting him for Fred, whom she claims as the father of her baby, and leaving the baby to scream while she goes out with him. It's Len hanging on as a lodger, still in love but forced to settle for the bleak, grudging familiarity her warring parents gradually admit him to. The baby dies, Fred ditches Pam; at the end the household sit in hopeless silence, Pam and her mother blankly facing the telly, Len mending a chair, the father bent over his pools devoutly as if inditing a letter to God.

Ronald Bryden, *New Statesman,* 12 Nov. 1965

I spent a lot of the first act shaking with claustrophobia and thinking I was going to be sick. The scene where a baby in a pram is pelted to death by a gang is nauseating. The swagger of the sex jokes is almost worse.

But it has to be said that this isn't a brutish play. It is a play about brutishness, which is something quite different. The swagger belongs to the characters, not the author. Edward Bond has planted a foul piece of social evidence in our files. If we prefer to turf it out I shan't be the least surprised, but it is a sizeable testimony. *Saved* is a study of reduction of personality that makes no excuses and offers no kicks, executed with a hard-headed humanity and a brazen technique ... about people who are at the very bottom end of human possibility. The well that most human beings drop down only through temper or drink or madness is the place where the characters spend their lives. They are thick, vengeful, incoherent, and terrified. They are frightened of one another but even more of themselves, because they have no insight and no sense of cause and effect.

The middle-aged couple in the play aren't on speaking terms, but they don't seem to be able to remember why, and no one thinks he can do anything about anything. The daughter treats herself as a thing that sex happens to; sex to her is a form of what she calls 'noseyness' creeping on her like a draught while she is buffing her nails. The only sort of order that any of the characters feel they can impose on life is the ritual of a fight. They call it 'getting sorted out'. But the ritual always fails, and their world flies apart; like lunatics or babies, their own violence makes them panic.

'Done now', says one of the gang while they are murdering the baby. The terrible point is that it isn't done at all, that there is still plenty of time to stop, but they are in such a frenzy of stupidity that they can see no difference between the past and the future. Everyone alive is tormented sometimes by the irreversibility of the past, but the people in *Saved* feel like this about the future as well, glaring at an avenue of blunders ahead that seem to them as uncontrollable as the ones that have already happened. . . .

Penelope Gilliatt, *The Observer,* 7 Nov. 1965

The most charitable interpretation of the play would be as a counterblast to theatrical fashion, stripping off the glamour to show that cruelty *is* disgusting and that domestic naturalism *is* boring. But the writing itself, with its self-admiring jokes and gloating approach to moments of brutality and erotic humiliation, does not support this view. In so far as the claustrophobically appropriate action has any larger repercussions, it amounts to a systematic degradation of the human animal.

Irving Wardle, *The Times,* 4 Nov. 1965

From first to last, Edward Bond's play is concerned with sexual and physical violence. It is peopled by characters who, almost without exception, are foul-mouthed, dirty-minded, illiterate, and barely to be judged on any recognizable human level at all. Nobody in his senses will deny that life in South London, or anywhere else for that matter, can be sordid, sleazy, and sinister. Nobody, furthermore, will deny that it is one of the functions of the theatre to reflect the horrific undercurrents of contemporary life. But it cannot be allowed, even in the name of freedom of speech, to do so without aim, purpose, or meaning.

Herbert Kretzmer, *Daily Express,* 4 Nov. 1965

I have had more vehement reactions about this play and what I wrote about it, pro and con, than about any other opening in the last year. The objectors mostly deny, with frightening violence, that such violence exists. Two people sent torn-up programmes. One enclosed a newspaper photograph of my child with her head cut off and daubed with red ink.

Penelope Gilliatt, *The Observer,* 14 Nov. 1965

Saved is not for children but it is for grown-ups, and the grown-ups of this country should have the courage to look at it; and if we do not find precisely the mirror held up to nature in which we can see ourselves, then at least we can experience the sacramental catharsis of a very chastening look at the sort of ground we have prepared for the next lot.

Laurence Olivier, letter to *The Observer,* 28 Nov. 1965

Early Morning

Play in twenty-one scenes.
Written: Jan. 1965-mid. 1967.
First London production: Royal Court Th., 31 Mar. 1968
(dir. William Gaskill; des. Deirdre Clancy; with Peter Eyre as Arthur, Moira Redmond as Queen Victoria, and Marianne Faithfull as Florence Nightingale).
First American production: La Mama Experimental Th. Club, New York, 18 Nov. 1970 (dir. Melvin Bernhardt).
Revived: Royal Court Th., 13 Mar. 1969 (dir. Gaskill, des. Clancy); Schauspielhaus, Zurich, 2 Oct. 1969 (dir. Peter Stein); Citizens' Th., Glasgow, 12 May 1974 (dir. Philip Prowse).
Published: London: Calder and Boyars, 1968; and in *Plays: One* (incorporating author's revisions).

In Early Morning *Edward Bond took the monumental human landmarks of Victorian England, those icons everyone knows from childhood – the unamused Queen herself, at all times in command of every situation however absurd or embarrassing; Albert, the Good, the ever-conscientious; Florence Nightingale, all propriety above the crinoline, and speculation below; bluff Gladstone, 'the people's William'; Disraeli with his affectations; and so on – took them and put them in totally unhistorical, bizarre, horrific situations, tranposing mental into physical cruelties. What you are seeing, he is surely saying, is our own aggressive, abrasive, callous, cannibalistic society with its roots in repression and emotional starvation.*

Bond's royal brothers, Arthur and George, are Siamese twins with but one heart between them. And it is Prince Arthur, locked in living hell with his 'heartless', spoiled brat of a brother, who makes the discovery that to possess that vital organ, to have pity for humanity in a world where 'aggression has become moralized and morality has become a form of violence' is to rock the boat, to become dangerous and therefore hunted down and killed.

17

The end of the play sees Arthur's apotheosis (presumably from one zone of 'heaven' to the next) rising slowly like a painted Christ, to a crescendo of the National Anthem, above the Royal tableau, posed as for the camera in that steely region where people eat people and 'feel no pain' ('Bon appetit', the Queen nods graciously between attacks with the Royal teeth on a bloody hand).

Cordelia Oliver, *The Guardian*, 14 May 1974
(on the Glasgow Citizens' production)

Saved was about the effect on its poorer members of a society which gives them nothing, teaching them only to take; a study in the emotional and cultural deprivation which lies behind the small items of mindless violence which fill up those newspaper columns not devoted to exhorting customers to consume. *Early Morning* extends the same image of Britain into a gargantuan Swiftian metaphor of universal consumption: a society based on cannibalism, in which all achievement, power, and even love consists of devouring other lives.

Bond comes from the class, still educated to margarine so that our meritocrats' paws may be buttered, whose lives were eaten by millions to build the Victorian Empire. It's natural for him to see the sooty bronze worthies who dominate our townscapes as the presiding deities of an anthropophagous religion of getting on: a mad Indian pantheon of voracious, many-armed gods in frock coats, dominated by the bombazined imperial Kali herself.

Ronald Bryden, *The Observer*, 14 Apr. 1968

The third act of Edward Bond's *Early Morning* . . . is unspeakably horrible in the undisciplined rapture with which it shows us Queen Victoria, Prince Albert, and their children revelling in cannibalism in heaven. *Early Morning* has presumably a savage moral purpose. It is like a nightmare dreamt by an overheated child whose head is a jumble of misunderstood fragments of what he has learnt from misguided elders about sex, religion, and the sort of history that is made up exclusively of palace intrigues, plots, murders, and wars . . . [A] melodramatic farrago of the deliberately disgusting and obscene . . . *Early Morning* has some things in it whose fineness is indisputable, notably the ambiguous and equivocal Saviour's bitter meditation on Hitler on the field of battle. But its horrors are altogether too much, even in the best of causes. As far as I could see the prolonged rending of human flesh in the last act did not produce sickness in any member of the first-night audience. But first-nighters are notoriously tough.

Harold Hobson, *Sunday Times,* 16 Mar. 1969

The whole play is written from [Arthur's] point of view, from his experience, so the audience has to understand this, the various stages that the character goes through, develops or discovers, the various freedoms it finds for itself. . . . I think *Early Morning* is essentially about working-class life. I mean, the plays that I am told are based on social realism very often seem to me the wildest fairy stories, and setting them against an immediately recognizable background doesn't make them any truer. So what I wanted to do in *Early Morning* was to take away all the known landmarks that might have led to false assumptions. It's like taking the labels off tins, so that you have to open them up to see what's inside — because so many of the labels were false anyway.

Bond, interviewed in *Theatre Quarterly,* No. 5 (1972)

Everything in the last act had to be very simple and direct — because in this act Arthur recovers his sanity; so the grotesque speeches belong to the middle act, in which he goes mad, and the first act, in which he is bewildered by the political set-up and his own emotional involvement in it — I mean that his ability to act freely had been stopped because his emotions had been seduced, and then he'd been morally blackmailed. In other words, he's been well brought up and then educated. His efforts to free himself are at first very awkward, because he's been smashed-up as a human being: so that at first he's driven to the fanaticism of the Queen, which is a sort of political madness — but he takes the Queen's philosophy to its conclusion. At the end of the second act he has a sudden insight into the truth about his own condition and the condition of society (you have to understand this relationship before you can act competently). He then sees himself and society clearer, relives the answers which had incapacitated him — and is freed.

Bond, letter to Michael Whitaker about the Royal Court production, 6 Nov. 1969

Only three Sunday performances could be given — otherwise police prosecution was inevitable. Because of rehearsing difficulties

(the actors were all earning their living in other rehearsals!) this
was cut down to two performances. One performance was given
– but after that the police visited the theatre, and the licensee
panicked and banned the second performance, and threatened to
have the police brought into the theatre. So a hurried performance
was given for the critics in the afternoon – and it was a disaster,
badly under-rehearsed and unconvincing. This isn't Bill Gaskill's
fault – if he'd had time it would have been one of his best productions. Inevitably, after this, the notices have been terrible –
but I don't care.

Bond, letter to Toby Cole, 8 Apr. 1968

Narrow Road to the Deep North

'A comedy' in two parts with an Introduction.
Written: Feb.-Apr. 1968.
First production: Belgrade Th., Coventry, 24 June 1968 (dir.
   Jane Howell, des. Hayden Griffin; with Peter Needham as
   Basho, Paul Howes as Kiro, and Edward Peel as Shogo),
   trans. to Royal Court Th., 19 Feb. 1969 (with Kenneth
   Cranham as Kiro).
First American production: Charles Playhouse, Boston, 30 Oct.
   1969 (dir. Louis Criss).
Revived: Kammerspiele, Munich, 2 Sept. 1969 (dir. Peter Zadek);
   Th. Royal, Bristol, 5 May 1971 (dir. Howard Davies).
Radio production: BBC Radio 3, 10 Aug. 1975 (dir. John
   Tydeman).
Published: London: Methuen, 1968; in *Plays and Players,* Sept.
   1968; and in *Plays: Two* (incorporating author's revisions).

*Bond found his theme in the writings of the Japanese poet, Matsuo
Basho [who] had written of finding a baby abandoned by its
parents near a river. Reflecting that the baby's suffering represents
the irresistible will of heaven, Basho left it and moved on. Nearly
three centuries later, Bond uses this incident as the prologue to
his play. Basho again leaves the child, taking the narrow road to
the deep north in order to pursue enlightenment instead of re-
maining to pursue humanity. When he returns, 30 years later
(which is three minutes after the play begins) the territory is
governed by a cruel and violent despot, Shogo, who, we learn at
the end, is the very child that Basho left behind. Shogo has built*

himself a city designed for perfection out of a neurotic need to create for himself some perceptible identity, to escape the feelings of chaos and emptiness which he feels beneath the surface of his life. Because his cruelty is arbitrary and compulsive, Shogo is . . . eventually overthrown. The forces of revolution represent a coalition between Basho and a pair of stranded British imperialists, a commodore with Rule Britannia for brain cells and his sister Georgina. . . . But the ruling powers of Christianity and British imperialism seem equally vicious and arbitrary and revolution is met with counter-revolution until madness, murder, and hypocrisy blend to form a lurid nightmare of authority. The play concerns itself with the evasion of one's humanity. . . . Even Kiro, the reflective young priest . . . commits suicide in despair at the end, and at the moment of death fails to stretch out a hand to help the naked, half-drowned man who is rising from the river.

Urjo Kareda, *Toronto Daily Star,* 29 Dec. 1971
(on the St. Lawrence Centre production)

Presented in Coventry last year, *Narrow Road to the Deep North* was the first Edward Bond play to reach the general public, presumably because it contains nothing likely to outrage them. Squeamishness apart (to which I plead guilty) there are other reasons for considering it his best piece so far. . . . It shows a big development in stylish identity and the relationship of form to content; it leaves you feeling that no one else could have written it.

Irving Wardle, *The Times,* 20 Feb. 1969

[The play] is the experience of life reduced, almost haiku-like, to a series of fragments, some of them almost arbitrarily side by side. Yet the fragments are beautifully, mysteriously fitted together in a general pattern. . . . The final image . . . is a haunting summation: a young priest falls on his ritual knife as a naked man, who has called for help from the river and has had to help himself, towels himself dry. Death crumples at stage right. Life wipes itself off in the background. The comment is as simple and pure as a . . . haiku.

Kevin Kelly, *Boston Globe,* 3 Nov. 1969
(on the Charles Playhouse, Boston, production)

[Reading the work of the Japanese poet, Bashō] I don't think I'd ever done it before, I just shut the book and I couldn't read it anymore. .... I more or less forgot about it but from time to time it came up in my mind and when I had this play to produce I just went back to the book and I read it, and wrote a play. ... I regard the play as critic fodder really. .... It's a very easy, light little play. In a sense I wrote it so quickly just to prove that I could do it ... because [the critics] just hadn't understood a word of the first performance of *Early Morning*.

Bond, speaking in 'The Lively Arts', BBC Radio 4, 26 Mar. 1969

A few nights ago we went to see some schoolchildren doing *Narrow Road* in an industrial part of Newcastle. They'd worked so hard and did it so well with [great] wit and integrity. ... The accent was so thick that I wouldn't have understood some of the play if I hadn't written it, but they were so full of life and intelligence. They have nothing, born in tarted-up slums and facing dead-end jobs. And yet they'd already understood so much about life. I felt extraordinarily lucky — to be able to write plays for such people.

Bond, letter to Margaret Ramsay, 7 Nov. 1977

Lear

Play in three acts.

Written: Oct. 1969 - early 1971.

First London production: Royal Court Th., 29 Sept. 1971
  (dir. William Gaskill; des. John Napier; with Harry Andrews as Lear, Celestine Randall as Cordelia, Carmel McSharry as Bodice, Rosemary McHale as Fontanelle, and Mark McManus as the Gravedigger's Boy).

First American Production: Yale Repertory Th., 13 Apr. 1973 (dir. David Giles).

Revived: Schiller Theater, Berlin, 4 June 1973 (dir. Hans Lietzau); T.N.P., Lyons, 8 Apr. 1975 (dir. Patrice Chéreau); The Other Place, Stratford, 18 June 1982 (dir. Barry Kyle; with Bob Peck as Lear, Alice Krige as Cordelia, Sarah Kestelman as Bodice, Jenny Agutter as Fontanelle, and Mark Rylance as the Gravedigger's Boy), trans. to The Pit, at the Barbican, 9 May 1983.

Published: London: Methuen, 1972 (with 'Author's Preface'); *Methuen Student Editions,* 1983; and in *Plays: Two.*

*When we first see Lear he is arriving at the border black with fury
to lash his men into speeding up work on a wall he is fanatically
erecting around his kingdom. . . . Only the two villainous sisters
are in attendance, renamed Bodice and Fontanelle; and . . . they
announce their forthcoming marriages to the two deadly enemies
against whom the wall is being built. The play thus starts with
civil war, and whatever Shakespearian plot material it contains is
shortly disposed of. The sisters are both bent on absolute power
and contemptuous of their husbands whom they speedily make
away with; while Lear, cast adrift from his army, wanders the
countryside in ragged incognito, witnessing Goya-like enormities
which befall all those who do him small acts of kindness, until he
and his daughters are captured by an insurrectionary peasant
army led by Cordelia (no relation). . . . Attended by the ghost of
a boy who sheltered him, Lear lives on as a captive of the new
regime, keeping his door open to any needy visitor, and finally
clambering to the top of the wall – on which the new regime is
working no less feverishly than the old – to dig two spadesful of
earth out of it before being shot down.*

*Bond himself has not changed; and we have no other play-
wright remotely like him. At first glance he seems totally lacking
in common humanity. But what passes for common humanity in
other writers can mean that they share our own compromising
attachments. . . .*

Irving Wardle, *The Times,* 30 Sept. 1971

It is unmistakably the work of a visionary craftsman. William
Gaskill has directed it as such and, given the large cast and the
cramped Royal Court stage, with remarkable fluency and effic-
iency. He has also invested it with striking visual images to match
the spare force of the text. The violence is not at all gloating; it
hurts, as it is meant to do, but there is no relish in it. As a result,
Lear, despite its unflinching brutality, is not a negative work. It
is a poetic indictment of what, in Bond's view, is wrong with our
world and our values. Although its tragic world is unimaginable
except in the theatre, it is not primarily a play for 'theatregoers'
but is meant for anyone concerned with our apparently hell-bent
course towards self-destruction.

Helen Dawson, *The Observer,* 3 Oct. 1971

'Edward Bond's *Lear* is magnificent' (Harold Hobson). But some critics have called Bond's *Lear* a 'failure'. Because it 'catalogues horrors'. Because it 'confuses' them. Don't be misled. Six years ago they said the same about Bond's *Saved* — and the Royal Court was prosecuted for it. Today *Saved* is a classic of the modern English theatre, performed in every capital in Europe. Five years from now the same will be true of *Lear*. Because it is a play of size and wisdom and theatrical daring. And because Edward Bond is a writer for our time. This World Premiere staging of his latest play has ten more days to run at the Royal Court. We urge you to see it for yourselves. You will be sorry if you miss it.

> Royal Court advertisement, *Evening Standard* (London),
> 20 Oct. 1971

What is unbearable about seeing Edward Bond's greatest (and biggest) play again, twelve years after its Royal Court premiere, is not the horrors and bleakness of war, the bayonettings and mutilations ... and the other brutalities that had members of Thursday night's audience carried out in seizures of shock. Not even the blinding of Lear by a time-serving prison doctor coolly demonstrating his 'scientific' removing device as if on television. It is the knowledge that it is even more topical now and will become more so as man's inhumanity gains subtle sophistication with the twenty-first century's approach. Barry Kyle's superb production makes one bitterly regret the Pit's limited capacity for those ignorant of this tremendous play.

> Anthony Masters, *The Times*, 21 May 1983

The reason I took *Lear* is that as a myth it seems central to people's experience. *Lear* is the family tragedy, magnified to the dimensions of political tragedy, state tragedy, and it seems to deal with very fundamental desires and fears that people have. It's a fascinating play — I mean Shakespeare's play — and I felt that somehow I wasn't living in the real world until I dealt with that myth in my own terms. In other words, Shakespeare's handling of that myth was no longer adequate for me, much as I admire that play. I think it's the greatest play written, and it's the play I get the most out of. Nevertheless, it doesn't work for me, and, in a sense, I have to criticize it.

> Bond, interviewed in *Performing Arts Journal*, I, 2 (Fall 1976)

Shakespeare's *Lear* is usually seen as an image of high, academic culture. The play is seen as a sublime action and the audience are expected to show the depth of their culture by the extent to which they penetrate its mysteries. ... But the social moral of Shakespeare's *Lear* is this: endure till in time the world will be made right. That's a dangerous moral for us. We have less time than Shakespeare. Time is running out. We have to have a culture that isn't an escape from the sordidness of society, the 'natural' sinfulness or violence of human nature, that isn't a way of learning how to endure our problems − but a way of solving them ...

My Lear makes a gesture in which he accepts responsibility for his life and commits himself to action. To the Egyptian, his death would seem sordid and futile, but not to the Greek. That is one sign of what I believe to be true: that human beings have continued, though unevenly, to increase their self-understanding. In our age, that development may be threatened once more by our increasing understanding of how to manipulate the physical world. A technocracy which is not a culture, which has abilities that are not directed by adequate ideas, is the worst of all barbarisms. The Christians were wrong in placing hell at one end of the universe and heaven at the other. Hell is a suburb of heaven, and on the way to heaven it is easy to stop for a rest and find you are in hell. My Lear's gesture mustn't be seen as final. That would make the play a part of the theatre of the absurd and that, like perverted science, is a reflection of no-culture. The human condition isn't absurd; it's only our society which is absurd. Lear is very old and has to die anyway. He makes his gesture only to those who are learning how to live.

> Bond, programme note for Liverpool Everyman Th.,
> production, Oct. 1975

In *Lear,* I make the king accept moral responsibility for his actions. In learning to understand himself he has become old and blind − nevertheless, he still acts. He sets an example, by doing this, to the young people who are left in his house at the end of the play − they are the really important people in the play − they represent for me a new possibility for change in society. They are my equivalent of Fortinbras, or the rulers who replace Shakespeare's Lear. When it came to practical politics, Shakespeare could only end his plays by reinstating the old order which would (I think) certainly replicate the old errors. *They* are not purified, only the dead victims are purified. What use is that as a guide to living?

> Bond, letter to Christine Meyerson, 28 Mar. 1977

What we have got to do is find some way of making people understand what the real situation is, and use their frustrations . . . not against scapegoats. *Lear* is a gesture. Our problem isn't a wall that we can dig up as Lear does. His action simply means that he understands the things he's done wrong in his life, and that he has to go back and undo them. If we can identify what our real dangers are, this is the only way I can see towards making genuinely revolutionary activity. You can't make a real revolution until you understand what the nature of the new revolution has to be — that is a revolution in an industrial society, which there's never been before.

Bond, interviewed in The Guardian, 29 Sept. 1971

Black Mass

Short play, part of *Sharpeville Sequence: a Scene, a Story and Three Poems.*

Written: early 1970.

First London production: Lyceum Th., 22 Mar. 1970 (dir. David Jones; with Kenneth Haigh, Diane Cilento, Freddie Jones, and Robert Lang).

Revived: Toneelgroep Centrum, Amsterdam, 20 Sept. 1971 (dir. Wim van de Grijn); Theater der Stadt, Bonn, Sept. 1972 (dir. Bohus Z. Rawik).

Published: London: Methuen (with *The Pope's Wedding),* 1971; in *Gambit,* No. 17 (1970); and in *Plays: Two.*

Lights up on an altar, above the altar a crucifix, Edward Bond himself hanging there as Jesus in loincloth. The South African Prime Minister has come to receive communion. . . . In bursts a police chief, interrupts the Minister. Emergency: the natives are gathering down the road, looking menacing . . . off the police chief goes, followed by riot troops. The communion continues. A shattering barrage of gunfire: Sharpeville has happened off-stage. The Prime Minister rushes out, followed by the priest. Jesus, alone, steps down off the cross, poisons the wine. The Minister returns, drinks the wine, dies . . . the only possible suspect is Jesus. He is expelled from the church; a riot cop, complete with helmet, boots, and goggles, is ordered to take his place on the cross. It is a Georg Grosz picture come to life, it is ghastly, it is the only possible kind of artistic imagery through

which to speak of such evil.
Michael Kustow, *The Listener,* 23 Apr. 1970

In a sense, writing shorter plays is like sharpening your pencil, putting a finer point on it again . . . it's very useful to take things down on to a smaller scale, structurally a smaller scale, so that one can experience almost within the grasp of one's hand the texture of a structure.
Bond, 'Conversation with Philip Roberts', British Council
Literature Study Aids (recorded 31 Mar. 1977)

Passion

'A Play for CND' in five scenes.
Written: early 1971.
First London production: Alexandra Park Racecourse, 11 Apr.
  1971 (dir. Bill Bryden; des. Di Seymour; with Nigel
  Hawthorne as the Prime Minister, Bob Hoskins as Buddha,
  and Penelope Wilton as the Queen).
First American production: Yale Repertory Th., 1 Feb. 1972
  (dir. Michael Posnick).
Revived: Downstage Th. Co., Wellington, New Zealand,
  18 Apr. 1976 (dir. John Banas).
Published: London: Methuen (with *Bingo),* 1975; in *Plays and
  Players,* June 1971; in *New York Times,* 15 Aug. 1971; and
  in *Plays: Two* (incorporating author's revisions).

An old woman – whose son is killed at the war – asks the Queen if she can have him back. The Queen requires the body for a monument, and at the unveiling launches an atomic onslaught in which the world is destroyed. Christ arrives but decides that when ordinary people suffer so much his small sacrifice is pointless. The old woman finds her son's body and he delivers a kind of elegy; and if you think that this is the sort of symbolic nonesense that half the earnest fools in Britain are writing you are probably right. But the earnest fools do not have Edward Bond's theatrical cunning; the quick statement of the theme, the very funny scenes with the Queen to hook the audience, the shock when the monument is revealed to be a crucified pig, and then the serious hammer blows. When Christ appears the dialogue mingles comedy

27

and high anger with absolute sureness.

Keith Dewhurst, *The Guardian,* 13 Apr. 1971

The Sea

'A comedy' in eight scenes.

Written: Apr. 1971 - Aug. 1972.

First London production: Royal Court Th., 22 May 1973 (dir. William Gaskill; des. Deirdre Clancy; with Simon Rouse as Willy, Diana Quick as Rose, Coral Browne as Mrs. Rafi, and Alan Webb as Evens).

First American production: Goodman Th., Chicago, 15 Nov. 1974 (dir. William Woodman).

Revived: Marlowe Th., Canterbury, 22 July 1975 (dir. David Carson); Teatro Duse, Genoa, 16 Dec. 1976 (dir. Armando Pugliese); Phoenix Th., Toronto, Apr. 1977 (dir. Graham Harley).

Television production: BBC Television, 5 Mar. 1978 (dir. Jane Howell).

Published: London: Methuen 1973, reprinted 1975 (with 'Author's Note for Programmes'); and in *Plays: Two* (incorporating author's revisions).

Mr. Bond's wit, that burgeoned in the dark corners of Saved *and* Lear, *here blossoms into full flower. He is witty in the way that Wilde and Shaw were witty, although the characters still inhabit the universe of his other plays, a bleak and harsh world where the weak are savaged by the strong and the strong misuse a power that depends upon the acquiescence of society as a whole. Set in a tiny English seaside village, it begins with a tempestuous storm and ends in sunlit calm with two young lovers breaking away from an isolated hierarchical society. This optimism is hardly total; the time is the early 1900s and we, at least, know that ahead of them lies a terrible war and, indeed, throughout the play gunfire pounds with the same relentless fury as the sea. The play deals with a classic class confrontation: Mrs. Rafi, a bullying* grande dame *with a coterie of simpering ladies, trampling on everyone's feelings because she feels they expect it, versus the village draper, Hatch, a sad, mad little man full of fears that visitors from outer space are stealing people's brains and replacing them with bits of machinery. The contest is, of course, an uneven one.*

John Walker, *International Herald Tribune,* 26 May 1973

After Bond's *Lear* (a truly great play totally misjudged by our squeamish critics who, in this case, seemed to be tone-deaf to great writing) one is tempted to think that *The Sea* might be something like his *Tempest.* ... But then, one could also argue that *The Sea* resumes the great solemn and violent theme of *Lear* and varies it in the mode of a scherzo. Hatch madly tramping along the shore, driven insane by the world's cruelty, is a harmless comic version of mad Lear, the stately Mrs. Rafi, statuesque queen-bee of her little seaside town and her rival and side-kick Mrs. Tilehouse, would then appear as attenuated versions of the wicked sisters, Bodice and Fontanelle, while the pure and perceptive girl, Rose Jones, who loses her fiancé in the storm and finally come to love his friend who was saved, has features of Bond's Cordelia. ... In both plays madness and the dehumanization of man are the main themes — on a heroic and barbaric scale in *Lear,* in the small domestic framework of the English class system in *The Sea.*

Martin Esslin, *Plays and Players,* July 1973

The [images] I had when I wrote *The Sea* go back to my childhood, the war. I was evacuated. Like now, the war was a time of great horror and fear. As if all the horrors on the movies were really coming to· life, happening. One afternoon, I remember so clearly being taken to a photographer's shop. By the coast. We were to have our photos taken dressed in sailors' costumes. The studio was upstairs. I remember looking out of the window. And there was this rather old-fashioned sort of camera, standing on its tripod, staring out to sea. I was a child. Little, about six. Suddenly I was up there at a giant's height, looking out. And I realized how vast the sea was. This enormous expanse of water. And suddenly all the dreadful things about war became very small.

The same afternoon I was told the story of somebody walking along the beach, finding the body of someone who had been torpedoed. Washed up. He'd tried to save his life by pulling his vest, his shirt, over his head. He'd died like that: with his hands sort of trapped above his head. It was one of those things when suddenly the world starts asking you questions. . . .

Bond, *Radio Times,* 4-10 Mar. 1978

It's essentially about life's problems and how we go about trying to sort them out. Like the sea, the problems come and wash over us, whether we want them or not. We cannot avoid them, we must needs deal with them. And, again like the sea, we come to grips with some of these problems, and some subside, again like the sea. It is also a play about insanity, chaos (as exemplified by Hatch and Mrs. Rafi), and sanity and ultimate serenity of mind (as partly shown by Evens). Yes, the play is strongly influenced structurally by Shakespeare's *Tempest*. I even have it start with a storm too. . . .

Willy and Rose are both part of the chaos and insanity at the play's start. But fortunately they do both get away from the town, which would have destroyed them in much the same way it ultimately destroys Hatch. What happens to poor Hatch? Oh, I imagine Mrs. Rafi pays for him to live out his life in an uncomfortable rest home somewhere nearby. Evens is closer to the same social level as Mrs. Rafi, despite his derelict condition. This is important, and explains why Mrs. Rafi treats him in some ways as an equal. Hollarcut is many social layers below them. There is no doubt but that Hatch is a Hitleresque concept. The cutting scene is the most difficult to stage. Ian Holm wanted a glove, it was such arduous work. The actor playing Hatch mustn't be obvious at all in this scene that he's cracking. It's a temptation to be avoided. . . .

PLEASE remember it is labelled A COMEDY and for a reason! It should be played lightly and with as much fun as possible. One of the German producers wanted to cut the final scene with Evens and Willy . . . and I gather they also worked for real water spouting from the corpse. All totally unnecessary, as I hope you agree. I structure my plays with infinite care. I know this one is tricky, with all its quick-changing scenes. It is very important that these shift quickly and easily to sustain the rhythm of the play. . . .

> Bond, letter to William Woodman, director of *The Sea*,
> Chicago, Nov. 1974

I left the last sentence of the play unfinished because the play can have no satisfactory solution at that stage. Rose and Willy have to go away and help to create a sane society – and it is for the audience to go away and complete the sentence in their own lives.

> Bond, letter to Tom. H. Wild for an amateur production
> in Reading, 16 Jan. 1977

Bingo

'Scenes of Money and Death': play in six scenes.

Written: Apr. 1973 - late 1973.

First production: Northcott Th., Exeter, 14 Nov. 1973 (dir. Jane Howell and John Dove; des; Hayden Griffin; with Bob Peck as Shakespeare), trans. to Royal Court Th., 14 Aug. 1974 (with John Gielgud as Shakespeare).

First American production: Playhouse, Cleveland, 31 Oct. 1975 (dir. Jonathan Bolt).

Revived: The Other Place, Stratford-upon-Avon, 3 Nov. 1976 (dir. Howard Davies; with Patrick Stewart as Shakespeare), trans. to The Warehouse, London, 8 Aug. 1977; Repertory Th., Seattle, 22 Feb. 1977 (dir. Robert Loper).

Published: London: Methuen, 1974 (with ('Introduction').

Spare, lean, poetic, yet rich in themes and ideas and full of suppressed agony and pain. . . . The governing theme of the play is the luxury of creativity in a world full of institutionalized violence; and it is typical of [Bond's] courage that the writer he has chosen to put in the dock is none other than Shakespeare. We see him in the last year of his life at New Place, Stratford, sitting pensively in his garden while local smallholders are ruined and common land enclosed, cutting himself off from the . . . terrors of the dark house and the detested wife and brooding on the cruelty of his age with its executions, its prisons, its public flogging, and its barbaric sports. . . . As he finally kills himself, he constantly cries 'Was anything done?' as if his whole life has been a failure to come to terms with the encircling evil. . . . Far from being a simplistic condemnation of the property-owning Shakespeare, it is a deeply moving study of the artist's impotence. . . . paradoxically, though the play is about the creative artist's limitations, it offers the exhilarating spectacle of a dramatist in full control of his talent.

Michael Billington, *The Guardian,* 15 Aug. 1974

Bond's play is itself a question: How could the man who wrote *King Lear,* the most searching and profoundly felt exploration in literature of human cruelty and injustice, have settled down in old age to be a burgher of Stratford, implicitly supporting and being supported by the dawning capitalist system at its greediest?

31

How could the poet who imagined the blinding of Gloucester and the old King plucking off his doublet to the storm, so as to learn the naked truth of man's condition, have become a pillar of provincial Elizabethan society; an unprotesting property owner living on rents, endorsing by his silence the brutal land enclosures and poor laws ... ? Bond's answer is that he could not — that Shakespeare ... could only survive by killing in himself the great and humane Shakespeare of the plays.

Ronald Bryden, *New York Times,* 25 Aug. 1974

[According to Garry O'Connor's review] Shakespeare's time ... was Italianate, 'florid, volatile, passionate, reflecting a highly volatile society'. Oh Christ. In the first place does he really mean, in the canon of Shakespeare's work, that there is no self-disgust, no doubt, that all this serenity and mindless 'genius', all plugged into this florid, passionate carry-on in the background? Are there no political references in the plays and poems, no references to bread shortages, unrest, disturbances, disgust, tension, fear of living? ... Shakespeare made it. When you survive ... you have choices. This play was the most tender, the most loving and affectionate treatment of a man who made it. Of his heart, which was in pain, because what he saw, too clearly, was a brutish and cruel world. ... The night I was there the Shakespeare I saw ... was hurt, disgusted, sorrowful, amused, self-disgusted, speculative, worried, afraid, benevolent, shrewd, depressed, tired, angelic. I saw the enactment of the character of a brilliant, impassioned, tender, articulate, complex man. ...

Pam Gems, letter to *Plays and Players,* Nov. 1974
(in response to O'Connor's review, Sept. 1974)

The play isn't telling any secrets. It tells what everybody knows about the way our wishes and intentions and consciences and ideas are turned awry — by money. WS's 'crime' isn't a very bad crime — he doesn't wilfully exploit anyone, or steal wilfully from them, or punish them for criticizing him, or claiming back their own things. It is all only part of his security and prosperity. ... The play is about the compromises WS makes. But what right has he to call on the poor to make these compromises? ... Even if he shows commercial restraint he still has to make compromises with his own humanity, his compassion. ... The crime relates to WS. It is brought out by his life. By his pact with society. Not a criticism of WS, because there is no alternative for him; other than hanging or beheading.

Bond, preliminary notes for *Bingo,* 4 Apr. 1973

Art has very practical consequences. Most 'cultural appreciation' ignores this and is no more relevant than a game of 'Bingo' and less honest.

Bond, *Sunday Times,* 25 Nov. 1973

I want to get away from the well-made play, and to do that I called *Bingo* 'scenes of something'. These scenes of something don't just tell a story, they also, I hope, make a statement to those watching, a statement the audience is invited to finish.

Bond, *New Haven Register,* 25 Jan. 1976

Why did *he* commit suicide? I don't know, perhaps because of that woman banging on the door. Well he had no reason to live. That's the judgement that one would make about him: that he had compromised himself so much, and, being an intelligent man, was aware of having compromised that much. You see, the imagery of that situation is extraordinary. Welcombe (the fields outside Stratford) was a sort of open heath. And he's written this play about Lear, who went mad on the heath, and standing on the heath insisted on certain moral insights, certain moral priorities for conduct, and you did those things even if it meant *your* death and even if it meant the destruction of your family. You did these things because there was no other life that is bearable. For Lear. And Shakespeare must have known that, otherwise he couldn't have written the play. That's what Shakespeare wanted, you know, otherwise you don't invent somebody like Lear as a fantasy, do you? You're saying something essential about what you demand and what you insist on, as the price or cost for being on this earth. And when it came down to his own business transactions he did exactly the opposite — he really did do the opposite. Of course, there's a lot of curfuffle about, 'you have no evidence to prove this' — but that is my whole point: *if* he had behaved as he should have done, as Lear told him he should have done, you would have known. . . .

I don't approve of the Son, no, because I think he deceives himself. Shakespeare acts fraudulently but he doesn't deceive himself mentally, he judges himself. The Son does not. He, I think, accepts a series of false values, false beliefs, false attitudes. I think he lies. And you've got to place these people in the historical context: it's absolutely true that these groups of people did go off and found America. And what good was that? I was writing the play when there was all this fuss about Nixon. So

... there's a moral deception also, in the Son. You see, he says at the end 'I killed him, I am guilty' — then three lines later he's saying he 'didn't kill him, perhaps it was somebody else'. And that also is self deception: he doesn't really accept the limitations that his situation imposes on him, and he fails to accept them in very much the same language that Shakespeare uses.

> Bond, in conversation with Howard Davies, director of *Bingo* at The Other Place, Nov. 1976, quoted in *Companion,*
> p. 57-63

The Fool

'Scenes of Bread and Love' play in eight scenes.
Written: Mar.-Oct. 1974.
First London production: Royal Court Th., 18 Nov. 1975
    (dir. Peter Gill, des. William Dudley; with Tom Courtenay
    as Clare, Bridget Turner as Patty, and Nigel Terry as Darkie).
First American production: Folger Th. Group, Washington,
    12 Oct. 1976 (dir. Louis W. Scheeder).
Revived: The Other Place, Stratford-upon-Avon, 25 June 1980
    (dir. Howard Davies; with James Hazeldine as Clare, Corrina
    Seddon as Patty, and Anton Lesser as Darkie), trans. to The
    Warehouse, London, 22 Sept. 1981.
Published: London: Methuen, 1976 (with 'Introduction' and
    'Clare Poems').

In his superb new play . . . Bond attains a new theatrical maturity. Luring his audience into the robust and violent rural world of John Clare, the farm labourer turned poet, at the beginning of England's industrialization in 1815, Bond creates a pageant of exploitation which demonstrates how imagination as well as manpower were victimized by the ruthless pursuit of profit. . . . The Fool *follows Clare's sad career from his life on the land to literary celebrity and finally, estranged from both land and literature, into madness. Shuffling uncomfortably between action and contemplation, the writer is a mercurial figure. Rarely the activist, the writer fashions himself in the centre of experience. With characteristic boldness, Bond dramatizes this aspect of Clare by first showing him on the periphery of events, dimly aware of the violence around him. Act I scarcely acknowledges*

Clare's calling, introducing him, instead, as part of a tatty band of farm labourers turned mummers who knock on the manor door at Christmas time to perform a rollicking song and play for small change and a hot meal. ... The festive charade is spoiled when one surly performer, Darkie, ... objects to the holiday platitudes and earns a lecture on economics from Lord Milton. ... With brilliant economy, Bond sets up the extremes of his debate and places Clare in the middle, assuaging Darkie who refuses Lord Milton's food. ... Act II opens with the startling image of a boxing match, the sound of flesh filtering through the shouts of the backers. In the foreground, Bond stages Clare as the centre-piece of London's literary arena. Like the boxers, Clare is surround-ed by his avid supporters who are turning him into a property. ... But, having transformed the chaos of life into well-wrought and marketable art, Clare finds himself a victim of the market-place ...

John Lahr, *Plays and Players*, Jan. 1976

You've got to be careful not to act the impact you know it's going to have on the audience. Like the prison scene. It's a dreadful situation, but you can't act that. Even though you're personally moved by it, you can't act it. So you act different moments within the scene. Like when I say John's poetry's going to be published. I'm happy about it. In the context, it makes the situation more moving. ... The audience react in a very strange way to Edward Bond. You feel that very strongly. You get no help from the audience. No feedback in the normal sense. You never feel you're in control of them. It's an odd experience. They don't seem to know how to react to Bond. They seem to be in awe of him. Often they react spontaneously, and then are surprised at the reaction that's just come out of them.

Bridget Turner (Patty in the Royal Court production), *Theatre Quarterly*, No. 21 (Spring 1976)

Clare is light, you see, and I deliberately chose the name Darkie — it's an invented name. ... Clare the poet, light, understanding, interpretation, and he doesn't want to use force because force ... isn't to do with that side of human behaviour which is to do with kindness and generosity and so on. ... Clare knows, for instance, that you can't change the world simply by smiling at it ... but if he uses just force ... all he will do is simply recreate the problem. And that is his dilemma . . . and so I showed Clare failing. . . . [He] is locked up in prison, just as Darkie's locked up in prison . . . both their lives are wasted and that's simply because the two necessary parts of action – understanding and whatever force is necessary to put that understanding into effect – are not joined.

Bond, unpublished interview with Salvatore Maiorana, Feb. 1981

A-A-America!

Double-bill of two short plays.

Grandma Faust: 'a burlesque' in three scenes.

Written: Jan.-Feb. 1976.

First performed: at the Almost Free Th., 25 Oct. 1976 (dir. Jack Emery; des. Norman Coates; with Henry Woolf, Don Warrington, Glen Walford, and Geraldine James.

The Swing: 'a documentary' in four scenes.

Written: Apr. - May 1976.

First performed: at the Almost Free Th., 22 Nov. 1976 (dir. Jack Emery; des. Norman Coates; with Henry Woolf, Don Warrington, Kevin Elyot and Ilona Linthwaite).

Revived: The Swing, Theater de Freien Hansestadt, Bremen, 15 Mar. 1977 (dir. W. Grimpe).

Published: London: Methuen, 1976, and 1981 (with 'Author's Note'); *Grandma Faust* also in *Fireweed* No. 5 (June 1976); 'The Swing Poems' published as a broadsheet in a limited edition of 1,000 by Inter-Action to coincide with the first production.

When asked to write for the American Connection season at the Almost Free, Bond delivered not one, but two plays. Collectively A-A-America! *(pronounced like a sneeze), both plays analyze the values that inform American society.* Grandma Faust *is a playfully cerebral cartoon in which Grandma, who is in fact the Devil, makes various bids through a hick Uncle Sam for the soul of Paul, a black man. . . .* The Swing *is Bond's most unambiguous and angry statement of outrage yet. At the end of* Grandma Faust, *Paul speaks a short coda which ends 'See you on the swing' . . . and there is an accompanying shift in style to a taut, etched naturalism. Paul tells the audience the historical details . . . In Kentucky in 1911, a black man was executed for murder. He was tied to a stake on the stage of the local theatre and the paying customers were allowed to shoot him dead. The more they paid, the more shots they got. The play begins just after the sale of a theatre ... to Skinner, a local merchant who intends to turn it into a store to catch the commercial boom that is about to transform the old Wild West. ... Skinner persuades the theatre owner's educated daughter [Greta] to take his son in hand. ... Skinner's shop is attacked, he is wounded, and in the general confusion, someone, possibly no one, touches Greta on the breast. ... Greta's sanity snaps, while Skinner dissolves into a vigilante fantasy world, accusing Paul and Paul's friend, Fred, of what has, in minutes, become a brutal rape. ... The sentenced victim is brought onto the stage [and] Bond here tugs away the last trace of predictable moral certainty because it is not Paul, the traditional victim, but Fred, and he is very, very white. ...*

To paraphrase the plot of *The Swing* is to fillet out a whole nervous system and leave a bag of bones. The richness and subtlety of the writing and the matching power of the dramatic structure unite to create a play that works like a sort of moral vaccine. By infecting the audience with some responsibility for the events, and confronting it with its own dark potential, the play seeks to generate antibodies against other, more immediate, plagues. ... It seemed wholly fitting that the play was applauded by its audience with silence.

Tony Coult, Plays and Players, Feb. 1977

Stone

'A short play' in seven scenes.
Written: Feb. -May 1976.
First London production: by Gay Sweatshop, at the Institute of Contemporary Arts, 8 June 1976 (dir. Gerald Chapman; des. Mary Moore; with Kevin Elyot, Tony Douse, Antony Sher, and Anna Nygh).
First American production: Ohio Performance Space, Manhattan, 27 Nov. 1981.
Published: London: Methuen (with *A-A-America!* and including 'Author's Note'), 1976.

Bond's Stone *is a vivid, assured, deceptively simple piece. It is*

*set in the traditional form of a parable. A young man enters
adulthood, full of hope ... carrying the seven gold talents his
thrifty parents have handed him. Through various encounters
he is burdened and corrupted until the final twist at the end of
his symbolic journey. What gives* Stone *its force is the outraged
humanity of its author, the dexterity of its language, and strength
of its theatrical images. Bond is not afraid to explore the simple
and the result is a compulsive piece of theatre.*

> Naseem Khan, *Evening Standard* (London), 11 June 1976

I do think you have to look for points of confrontation, but it's
difficult because they get out of hand. But there must be those
situations where oppression is made to identify itself. You must
tread on its toes and make it declare itself.

> Bond, *Gay News,* 17-30 June 1976

The Woman

'Scenes of War and Freedom': play in two parts and twenty-three
   scenes.
Written: Mar. 1974-June 1977.
First London production: National Th., 10 Aug. 1978 (dir. Bond;
   des. Hayden Griffin; with Yvonne Bryceland as Hecuba,
   Nicky Henson as Heros, Susan Fleetwood as Ismene, and Paul
   Freeman as The Dark Man).
Published: London: Methuen, 1979 (with 'Poems, Stories, and
   Essays').

*Part One consists of fourteen scenes set in a range of locations in
the Greek camp outside Troy and in the city itself. The action ...
encompasses the final stages of the siege; Priam is already dead,
and power passes briefly to Hecuba. ... In Bond's treatment of
the war, the prize is not Helen but a stone image of the goddess
Fortune, once the property of the Athenians. ... Heros, the
Athenian commander, ... resists the logic of a solution devised
jointly by Hecuba and by his own wife, Ismene, whereby the
statue would be surrendered and Troy spared. The troops must
have their due: carnage inevitably ensues. ... Part Two ... is
located on an unidentified island. ... Hecuba and Ismene, now*

blind and insane respectively, have been shipwrecked ... and the stone goddess lost on the seabed. Still seeking the statue, the Athenians hunt the woman down and compel the islanders to cast nets for it. ... Heros becomes obsessed with the need to recover the statue. Hecuba, in alliance with the Dark Man, a refugee from the Athenian silver mines,contrives Heros's death and delivers the island from Athenian occupation. Hecuba dies in a great storm and the islanders resume their lives.

The Woman, Bond has indicated, may be regarded as a summing-up of all his previous work; as such it restates his ongoing preoccupations and reaffirms the values which underlie them. ... As in *Lear,* insanity and the limitation of personal freedom are presented as functions of the industrial-military ethic. As in *Saved,* a simple act of casual brutality suggests a thousand others; like the stoning of a baby in its pram in the earlier play, the death of Astynax serves as a dramatic metaphor of society's violence against the weak. ...

The emphasis placed upon sexual politics ... constitutes a new departure for Bond. Sexism is treated as one more form of social violence here, and is not to be set apart from the wider political analysis. Thus it is the women who urge a peaceful resolution of the conflict at Troy. ... Moreover, it is Hecuba who perceives the hopeless logic of attrition, and Ismene who is used to puncture the heroic posturing of the old school of warriors, as embodied by Nestor, and to reveal the Realpolitik of the succeeding generation for what it is. ...

Hecuba supplies the play with its structural spine and acts as its expositor. ... She reflects upon, and articulates the significance of, the developing action. ... She is also instrumental in shaping this. ... Heros dies because she has absorbed the lesson ... if we cannot change a social system which militates against a just and non-violent mode of life, then we shall destroy ourselves.

George Savona, *Gambit,* No. 36 (1980)

Bond has now adopted the role of a revolutionary artist; and however potently Greek myths condition modern imagination, they tend to create imprisoning structures asserting a defeatist view of the world. Bond has never shown much respect for postures of sublime despair, and he has now taken a crowbar to the great Attic Bastille, with the aim of releasing its mighty victims into a new world where they stand some chance of survival if they use their wits.

And, as in the case of *Lear*, it is in no way diminished by comparison with its mighty prototype. It takes an author of commanding powers to modulate from the bloody excesses of the first act to the ironic realism of the second without crashing his gears: and the tonal variety of the second act varies from passages of magnificent rhetoric, such as the cripple's set piece on the mines, to outright farce, where he shows his affection for the two tragic ladies by flooring them for a merciless tickling.

Irving Wardle, *The Times,* 11 Aug. 1978

I'm pretty sure I remember what happened. I'd had *The Woman* in my mind for some time and had thought that would be the next play I would write. Then the idea of Clare intervened. I thought I ought to do *The Woman* first — as I'd been considering it and so had some ideas and I thought it would be complicated to start something from the beginning on top of this. Nevertheless the Clare play seemed more immediate in that it was simpler to do. So I wrote down all that I then knew about *The Woman* (I'd avoided doing this so far) so that it would remain clear in my head. Then I mapped out a possible shape for Clare. ... It seemed to me, after I'd done it, that I had the makings of a Clare play. So I decided to put *The Woman* on one side and concentrate on Clare.

Bond, letter to Malcolm Hay, 7 Nov. 1978

The play falls into two parts. In the first part you see people at war — people in conflict. ... I mean, neither is right, neither is wrong. It's just a struggle for power, possession, within two imperialist powers. One — which is losing its authority — is in descent and another which is in the ascendency. It's Athens and Troy. And that simply looks at the nature of war and the suffering it causes and it tries to get away from the monolithic idea of a war fought between two nations which are equally united within themselves; and so I look at the wide range of Troyan society. You see the people — the proletariat — who are locked up in the city and you see their attitude to the war and you see the rulers of that city. And with the Greeks, I look at the Army and — at all levels — at the Supreme Council and also at the sentries on duty so that you then see the class relationships within those countries and the way they work and you can look at the problem of whether or not the war is to the advantage of everybody or not. The soldiers because they've been there for a long time, have, in fact, got Troyan girl-friends and, in fact, have Troyan children. That's the first part of the play. . . .

In the second half of the play, I move into a development from the first half and I look at the conflict within . . . any social structure in history. The sort of story-telling changes because the figures there become emblematic and I tell the story in a different way. . . . I'm telling a story about history. Now, the first act is a moment in history and the second half is a story about history — 'step further away and look at all history, see if you can discern patterns in history' — and that makes a demand on an audience, but I think that's a good demand. . . . What happens in the second half is that figures represent various forces in history and what they have to do in the second half is defeat the Greek general. Now, the Greek general, as in all reactionary societies, has a false ideal which is described in the play as a statue which he has to search for, and all fascist societies have some sort of golden age mythology or some ideal like that — he's always searching for this ideal which, of course, he can never attain. It doesn't exist. The statue has actually been lost at sea and this absurd man . . . says, 'Oh, well, that's all right, we'll just fish the sea'; and so he sends all these fishing boats out with nets to find the statue and that's fine, but you see the trouble is that he then starts saying 'Well, wait a moment, those fishermen aren't fishing properly and they're lying to me and I will kill them and I will punish them and so on', so that you see how the irrational creates terror within a society.

Well, the whole object is to defeat this man . . . and this is achieved by the combined forces of an escaped miner and of Hecuba. The escaped miner comes from a more advanced proletariat. So I showed the two forms of proletariat on the stage — the primitive farming, fishing form, and the advanced industrialized form, and there's Hecuba, who I take to represent history and she is able to understand what's going on. Heros doesn't understand what's going on. He's totally irrational, but Hecuba understands. . . . And if I say that history is the battle between the rational and the irrational, well, then, Hecuba stands for the rational and the combination of the rational and the proletariat triumphs. In the play necessarily they're divided into two characters, but when we talk about movements in history we're not talking about characters, we're talking about masses.

Bond, in an unpublished interview with Salvatore Maiorana,
Feb. 1981

The Bundle

'Scenes of Right and Evil, or New Narrow Road to the Deep
   North': play in ten scenes.
Written: July-Oct. 1977.
First London production: The Warehouse, 13 Jan. 1978 (dir.
   Howard Davies, des. Chris Dyer; with Bob Peck as the
   Ferryman, Patrick Stewart as Basho, Mike Gwilym as Wang,
   and Paul Moriarty as Tiger).
Published: London: Methuen, 1978 (with 'The Bundle Poems'
   and 'A Note on Dramatic Method').

Like his earlier Narrow Road to the Deep North, *this work opens
with the great seventeenth-century poet Basho refusing to care
for an abandoned child – the bundle – as he sets off in search of
enlightenment. In the 1968 play, the child grows up to be a
tyrant. In* The Bundle ... *the child Wang becomes a liberation
leader. Bond ... has progressed from exposing the condition of
our times to showing the possibility of, and the need for, changing
that condition. And it is a condition of cruel exploitation that
Bond depicts, with his characters oppressed by men – the landlord
– and by nature – the river that floods. Yet, as Wang grows up,
Bond shows with humour and relentless integrity the villagers
learning to overcome both, learning to take control of their
lives. After Basho leaves the bundle, a ferryman takes up Wang
... yet, as the price of saving the family from drowning, he is
bartered into the service of the poet who has returned to become
a local judge, having found personal enlightenment. ... Wang
organizes a group of bandits and leads an armed struggle which
forces the landlord, who has abandoned Basho, to retreat to the
provincial capital. Basho's palace is sacked, and he stomps around
in tatters asking the way to the deep north while the villagers
stand together in a demonstration of the power of collective
strength.*

Colin Chambers, *Morning Star,* 19 Jan. 1978

Like *Lear* it has the force and the onward movement of a tidal
wave. It communicates narrative joy; a complicated tale is to be
told, spanning many years, and the playwright's craft in keeping
us aware of our bearings is immaculate. Necessarily he writes

many scenes, but he gives each one a shape and a dynamic. . .
Mr. Bond returns us to the weight and rhythm of epic theatre.
Robert Cushman, *The Observer*, 22 Jan. 1978

The Bundle is set in a primitive Asian community. It will be said
that this is another way of 'exporting your conscience' — just as it
has been said I ignore the present when I sometimes write about
the past. Reaction likes to keep its hand on the past because it
throws too much light on the present. I chose the Asian setting
because it enabled me to abstract certain social forces and show
their effect in a direct and simple way.

Voltaire did the same. In art distance sometimes lends clarity.
The people in *The Bundle* live by a river. Directly or indirectly
they all live from it. From time to time it floods and destroys
them. If, as the play invites, you substitute factories and offices —
all industrialism — for the river, then my purpose is plain.
Bond, *The Guardian*, 13 Jan. 1978

I remember I once heard [Bond] give a note to another member
of the cast. . . . He suggested that she try to deliver [a speech] as
if she were standing about six feet behind herself, looking at herself as she was saying it. That sort of technique does often apply
in performing a play by Bond. I have found that the scenes which
haven't worked in some performances of *The Bundle* were those
when I was pushing at the emotion rather than playing the ration-
ality and logic of the lines.
Mike Gwilym (Wang in the Warehouse production),
interviewed by Malcolm Hay, 20 Jan. 1978; quoted in
Hay and Roberts, p.278

The whole play begins from that basic image [of the bundle]. It's
a given. The story of Basho seeing the child and then going on is
not my story. It is in Basho's autobiography. I think that it is
such an extraordinary incident. That is given as it were in the
subject. I arrived very early on at the idea of the curlew, for
instance, as being something that speaks to the Ferryman and
makes him go back. I suppose the same sort of area is that Tiger
only has one hand. I wanted to show physically on stage that he
was an incapacitated person; that there were certain things that
he could do and do very well. I don't agree with the view that
says that Wang has been turned into someone who cannot act and

Tiger is someone who can act. . . . Wang does act. He has become a creator of his society through his experience. He combines action with rational concepts and when that happens then things can become truly creative. Tiger really only has actions and a form of opportunism. So he is not really an actor. There is very little he can do. He doesn't have concepts that interpret his experience in the way that Wang has, and in order to show this I cut off his hand. . . .

Basho and the Ferryman both have sticks in the opening scene because they are both setting out on a journey. The Ferryman by taking the child is setting out on a journey to rediscover his life. His life is completely changed by the child. One is setting out on the river which is in a creative vein, the other is setting out on a road which seems to take him through a series of charnel houses, if you believe what he says. He ends up wrapping his feet with cloth that was used to bind corpses' mouths. I use the idea of the mouth and drinking throughout the whole play. At the end of the play, though the structure of the Warehouse theatre in London made it impossible, it would have been better if Basho could have done what the script says – that he actually went in among the audience. The idea of the stick at that point in the play was that he would be completely collapsed on the stick, almost like a bundle at the bottom of the stick, as if the stick was pointing at him or making him.

Bond, quoted in Peter Hulton,
Dartington Theatre Papers, Second Series, 1978

The Worlds

Play in two parts and twelve scenes.
Written: Oct. 1977-Mar. 1979.
First production: Newcastle Playhouse, 8 Mar. 1979 (dir. Bond; des. Hayden Griffin; with an amateur cast). Re-directed by Bond, for Activists' Youth Th. Club, Royal Court Th. Upstairs, 21 Nov. 1979.
First professional production: New Half Moon Th., 12 June 1981 (dir. Nick Hamm; des. Sue Blane; with Ian McDiarmid as Trench and Terry).
Published: London: Methuen, 1980 (with *The Activists Papers*).

On a bare stage covered in white tarpaulin, the company directors gather to toast 25 years of successful business while the 4,000-

strong work force is on strike demanding a 30 per cent wage increase. After drinks, back-slapping, and a discussion on how a man may learn to trust himself, the managing director, Trench, is abducted by terrorists while reading poetry. . . . When freed, Trench finds himself ousted in a boardroom putsch. . . . Trench invites his colleagues and their wives to a final dinner at his country house where he is to unveil a painting of the Board. Trench uses the occasion to flail the world that has victimized him: with a flourish, he unveils a joke fairground painting with two holes for the heads of plump bathers. In a magnificently hysterical climax, one of the directors sobs uncontrollably while one of the wives strips provocatively. The surface cracks.

By this time, we have met Bond's chief character, Terry, a union militant. Terry moves centre-stage in the second act, where another kidnap – of a company chauffeur – is unrelated to wage demands. For the directors and the police, the strikers and the terrorists are one and the same thing. . . . Terry refuses to toe a humanitarian line and end the strike in exchange for the chauffeur's life. . . . Bond gives a girl terrorist a long speech about the two worlds, defined as the world of appearance and the world of reality. In the first, she says, there is right and wrong, the law and good manners. In the second, which controls the first, machines and power. . . . She then disappears with the rest and Trench shoots the bandaged chauffeur. Finally, Terry, with his wife and baby, sits on a park bench. . . . Terry, not the girl, suggests Bond, is the true revolutionary.

Michael Coveney, *Financial Times,* 10 Mar. 1979

It's a more pictorial play. . . . Most people, you see, when they're on stage are making a commentary about themselves. . . . Hamlet uses his voice as a commentary about what's going on inside Hamlet. The relationship is between the words and the hidden subjective self. The subjectivity of the character is allowed to speak. What I am moving towards is not for one moment to deny the subjectivity of the character because I think that's very important, but I'm trying to move towards a theatre in which very often the character is not relating the voice to himself but is relating his voice, his words, to the 'pictoriality', the picture of the whole stage. . . . It's like the moment when the leading working-class agitator in *The Worlds* sits at the businessman's table. He's put in an unusual situation − he's there in his overalls and he's sitting at the chairman's desk and behaving like neither of the two characters you see, but talking in relation to a new image being shown on the stage. This is a more objective way of describing the way history moves − of describing the political relationships between people. . . . What we've got to do is try and . . . find a way of writing plays where the characters can exercise being agents of the future. . . . Instead of having a soliloquy, the character, as it were, gathers himself up into a position of authority and power and speaks with the authority of history. . . . A public soliloquy − that's what I call these modes when people talk objectively. . . .

[Trench] doesn't see himself as a vulgar businessman out to grab money − he's very interested in all that; but he does see himself as a renaissance princeling, if you like − a real gentleman in that way. Fine . . . except that he's born four or five hundred years too late and he gets himself in the situation where the law is used against him. He gets himself ousted, removed from power by his colleagues simply manipulating the business laws. You often hear about conflicts in the board-room and so on . . . it's that sort of thing and he has to be absent from his firm for quite a while: he's actually made a hostage. And while he's away he loses his job . . . and it's his whole life. . . . The culture that's based on it also collapses and that's as much as to say that he goes through a psychological crisis, that his politico-psychology collapses with his culture, and what happens is that he goes through a process of increasing nihilism. He has nothing natural to fall back on − no natural instincts, no natural propensities, no natural goodness or anything like that, and so he gets increasingly more interested in destruction and increasingly more dangerous and he ends up by imagining, by simply spending his time having day-dreams, reveries, about the release of the H-bombs. In a way he's a sort of summary figure like the figures in the second act of *The Woman*. He is an individual but he also represents a particular tendency in society of increasing cynicism, of increasing destructiveness, of increasing barbarity; and he demonstrates the way these things happen in subjective political terms, in the politico-psychology.

Bond, in an unpublished interview with
Salvatore Maiorana, Feb. 1981

If you take something like *The Worlds*: it's a highly emotional play. I don't like debate plays. My plays are not Shavian. The characters don't actually sit down and debate things. They have strong emotions – the characters fall in and out of love. They hate, they murder. . . . Nevertheless it is a rational theatre in the sense that I do not see human beings as creatures who inherit their nature from the past.

Bond, in an unpublished interview
with Nick Philippou, Dec. 1982

Restoration

'A Pastoral' in two parts and twelve scenes.
Written: July 1979-Oct. 1980.
First London production: Royal Court Th., 21 July 1981 (dir.
   Edward Bond; des. Hayden Griffin and Gemma Jackson; music
   by Nick Bicât; with Simon Callow as Lord Are, Philip Davis as
   Bob, and Debbie Bishop as Rose).
Published: London: Methuen, 1981 (Royal Court Writers Series),
   revised version, 1982.

We are in eighteenth-century England: a world of cruelty, injustice, and iron privilege. Indeed the action hinges on Lord Are's casual murder over breakfast of his unwanted wife, a mineowner's daughter whom he has married for money. Having dispatched his wife with foppish indolence, Lord Are then seeks to pin the deed on a guileless, illiterate footman, Bob Hedges. And the rest of the play consists of a battle between Bob's black, justice-hungry wife and the fortified privilege of aristocracy. Simply stated, it sounds like a conflict between good and evil, the exploited and the exploiter. But Bond is cleverer than that. For a start he makes Bob a stubbornly hypocritical peasant lad who willingly shops a fellow footman caught stealing the silver. In one extraordinarily powerful scene we see Bob tying his colleague to a chair and bundling him into a chest. So, by a fine irony, Bob, the victim of injustice, is himself a boss's man. . . .

At the bottom of it all I suspect Bond is saying something straightforward: that justice is every man's right but a caste system's plaything. But what is heartening is that he gets right away from the playing-card simplicities of agitprop and that he makes his points through laughter. . . . If there is a problem, it is that there is almost too much to digest at one sitting (but when could one last say that of a new play?).

Michael Billington, *The Guardian,* 22 July 1981

In many ways, *Restoration* is closest in Bond's work to *The Fool.* . . . It shares the same affectionate but unsentimentalized fascination with the East Anglian rural working class of the eighteenth century, the same horror at the identification of justice with the rights of the landowners, the same distress at the consequences of the servants' humiliating subservience to that powerful hierarchy. *The Fool* explored the ground through the perspective offered by the life of John Clare, the peasant as poet. *Restoration* turns from the writer to a literary form, Restoration comedy. . . .

Restoration has fragments of social detail that are brilliantly observed. He is particularly acute in a scene where Bob and his mother want to turn in another servant, Frank, for stealing one of Lord Are's spoons. Frank's city-bred belief in the servant's right to steal anything his master might leave lying around is set against Bob's obstinate sense of inherited duty to the Are family. . . . Bond refuses to treat the servants as an undifferentiated group. Instead, scenes like this establish a vast number of deep divisions: city against country, indoor servants against outdoor, black against white, old against young.

For some years now Bond has accompanied his plays by sequences of poems designed to explicate the events of the plays. For *Restoration* he has incorporated the poems into the play itself as songs with music by Nick Bicât. They have clear echoes of the Brecht-Eisler style, punctuating and commenting on the action through poetic analogues and modern parallels.

Peter Holland, *Times Literary Supplement,* 7 Aug. 1981

The second half is different from the first half and has to be. . . . The first is easier to understand. But the second half is just as important. It tells its story by exposing different attitudes to the main theme. . . . The second half concerns the creation of a new Lord Are – his alliance with Hardache was the basis for the English eighteenth century. His dementia in Scene 10 is the basis for modern fascism – which is a corruption of his alliance with Hardache. In other words, the play points at us from the eighteenth century and into the modern world. In doing this, it joins up with the songs. I have to make a demand on the audience that they follow this.

> Edward Bond, letter to Margaret Ramsay, 30 July 1981

I was deeply depressed over the last [1979] election and, indeed, I wrote *Restoration* as a consequence. I saw Bob as being the typical, working-class Tory voter, and the play is about his betrayal. Then I looked around for what I thought would be hopeful conflicts, conflicts that would perhaps rescue him from his fate. And I thought that in the racist conflict could be found a very good and informed political confrontation – a rational response to irrationality. So the play now couldn't be more topical. . . . Violent confrontation *is* inevitable if you are forced to live irrationally. Because it is the only way things will change. . . . We haven't yet found a way of change by using our minds.

> Bond, *The Guardian*, 31 July 1981

Summer

'A European Play' in seven scenes.

Written: Apr. 1980-Jan. 1981.

First London production: National Th., 27 Jan. 1982 (dir. Bond; des. Hayden Griffin; with Yvonne Bryceland as Marthe and Anna Massey as Xenia).

First American production: Manhattan Th. Club, 19 Feb. 1983 (dir. Douglas Hughes).

Radio production: adapted by Bond, BBC Radio 3, 23 Dec. 1982 (dir. Anthony Vivis).

Published: London: Methuen, 1982 (New Theatrescript), revised edition, 1982 (includes poems, fables, and 'Service', a story).

Edward Bond's new play . . . is set in an unnamed country which seems to be Yugoslavia; a sunny Mediterranean land with a growing tourist industry, occupied by the Germans during the war and subject to a social revolution after it. Three middle-aged survivors of that distant time confront the past and each other. Xenia . . . is a member of the ousted ruling class who now lives in London but spends each summer in the house that was once the family home; Marthe . . . , formerly a servant in her household, is caretaker and part-owner of that house; the third survivor is a comic German

49

tourist·from the new hotel who, as a member of the occupying force during the war, had shot hostages in the island prison camp in which Xenia's father later died. Marthe has only a few days left to live and faces death with peasant stoicism. Her son David . . . , a doctor, spells it out to Xenia, who refuses to accept it. The two women are both united and divided by a shared past. Although Xenia saved Marthe's life when she was arrested by the Germans, Marthe later gave evidence against Xenia's father when he was tried and imprisoned by the Communists. Xenia's father had been a good man, liberal and kind. Kindness is not enough, spits Marthe, the world requires justice, and her mood, the mood of the play, implies that she and her countrymen have now found it. While the two ageing women rake over the ashes of old battles, their children, Ann . . . and David, fall in love and the world seems, through their eyes and ours, fresh and new, their elders' anger and bitterness become sad and rather comic. Unnecessary, as far as they are concerned.

When Bond is producing his best work, as in this play, his debt to Shakespeare is both obvious and enriching. Apart from his use of poetic imagery, he gives us a sense of action taking place at several levels and, perhaps most important of all, that a tension between irreconcilable opposites is of the very essence of drama. Tensions are manifold: between order and anarchy, justice and mercy, and − in this particular play − between life and death, light and dark: Marthe is dying, and tells us that it is death which gives us our enjoyment of life. The physical emphasis in the play is on such things as light, warmth, simple pleasures: the remembered horrors are all in people's heads, and in their speeches.

Summer is a modern rendering of *The Tempest*: the age-old quarrel between the exiled dispossessed Prospero and his kinsman is enacted by Xenia and Marthe; the boorish German soldier turned tourist with an appetite for sandwiches and ladies in bathing costumes is Caliban; and Ann and David are Ferdinand and Miranda. . . . The German tourist tells a frozen-faced Xenia of the horrors that took place on the island beach on which they now sunbathe: the sunny cliff once an execution wall, corpses floating in the sea. Afterwards Ann and David exclaim on the beauty of the place, which has now become a shrine to their love.

Eva Figes, *Times Literary Supplement*, 5 Feb. 1982

Xenia is like an Oedipus. She always returns. Even at the end she comes back as a figure of force. It's now her automatic reflex: she always wants to know the truth even if it will destroy her, because she cannot live without her version of the truth — which is a lie — and she demands that others corroborate it for her. I suppose Marthe is like a Sphinx to her. But Marthe would say — rightly — that there is no mystery: the truth is on the surface and it's only lies that need to be profound and hidden. . . . Try to follow the patterns of certain speeches: the Sun speech, for example, which recurs and is developed throughout the play — starting as lights on fishing boats, reaching a climax with Marthe's sun speech — and then becoming simple action in the breakfast laying (the daily meal that celebrates dawn).

The girl is a difficult part. It has to be highly dramatic. In the beginning, she's almost neurotic, comatose: she decides at the last minute on the plan not to sleep with David. It's like putting a pistol to her head to see what will happen. But there is no conventional love scene. . . . Instead (apart from the dramatization of her reaction to the voices off in Scene 2) you only see the completed change — not the process of change — at the end of Scene 4. When David says: 'This island is sacred to us' — the audience ought to want to cheer! It is the most natural and complete statement — what the sun says to the dark. . . . And so the island belongs to David and Ann. But they can't inherit it from Marthe: they must also struggle. So they say, we will fall in love and then part. And in the final scene they dare each other to accept this challenge — and they accept it. . . .

Xenia has to be played seriously . . . but in Scene 6 she is out of a farce: the judgement has been passed. In Scene 6 she has no sympathy for the situation, she has all the automatic behaviour of a farcical figure — even to theatre business with flowers. This applies in other ways to the German — he comes on as a figure of comedy — yet he has the most poetic of speeches (we called it the ghost speech — the ghosts rise up out of the sea to accuse him . . .); yet he too ends in farce.

Bond, letter to Kim Dambaek, Aalborg Teater,
Denmark, 4 Jan. 1983

Derek

A short play in 'Seven Incidents'.
Written: Sept. 1982.
First production: The Other Place, Stratford-upon-Avon, 18 Oct.

1982 (dir. Nick Hamm; des. Jill Jowitt).
Published: London: Methuen, 1983.

A story of Derek, a working-class boy with a brilliant mathematical brain, who is persuaded, in order to avoid a long prison sentence for opening a safe, to undergo a brain transplant. The brain he receives is Biff's who, after Eton and Sandhurst, is refused the safe parliamentary seat which has been in the family for generations, on the grounds that he has a mental age of ten. Biff, with Derek's brain, enters Parliament on the law-and-order ticket. Derek, in a wheelchair after the operation, is cheated of money promised to him by Biff. When he recovers, he joins the army and, like his father before him, is killed on active service.

I've just come back from three days at Stratford with the RSC. The little play – it's called *Derek* – is coming along well. I enjoyed working with the actors. They were very co-operative and helpful – and very quick at understanding. They've all worked incredibly hard – either acting or performing every day and every evening. Officially they're supposed to get a day off – yet they were even asking me to work with them through their lunch breaks and rest periods. We took time off for a demo on the day of action – marched through Stratford with placards and Dame Peggy at the head of the line. I told them they ought to have worn their costumes . . .

Bond, letter to Margaret Ramsay, 24 Sept. 1982

Red Black and Ignorant

Short play.
Written: Dec. 1983-Jan. 1984.
First London production: Barbican Th., 19 Jan. 1984 (dir. and des. Nick Hamm).
Unpublished.

When I was asked to write for 'Thoughtcrimes' at the Barbican, I decided to write about nuclear war. A society which does not 'know itself' does not act rationally. If the processes by which the state organizes society's various strata and activities are corrup-

*tions of the truth, then these corruptions will affect all its deci-
sions, little and great. I created a character who in fact never lives:
he is burned in the womb in a nuclear war. His 'ghost' comments
on the people who, to preserve freedom, condemned him and
millions of others to the perpetual imprisonment of death. He
argues that a society that invests and labours to make that
possible, and gambles on having to do it, ought not to be called
civilization. That would be the greatest double-think. It should be
given its proper name: barbarism.*

Bond, *The Guardian,* 16 Jan. 1984

The Tin Can People

'A short play' in three sections.
First production: by Bread and Circuses Th. Company, Cannon
   Hill Arts Centre, Birmingham, 4 May 1984 (dir. Nick
   Philippou).
Unpublished.

*A few survivors of nuclear war come together in a valley where
five great storehouses were exposed to a neutron bomb. Their
contents, millions of tins of food, remain undamaged, and the
survivors live out of the tins for years. A stranger, alone for seven-
teen years, comes to the community and is suspected of bringing
a new disease. The group debates the course of action to take as
some of its members die and begin to develop once again the
means of killing. Gradually, the deaths cease, the stranger is
absorbed into the community, and they begin to contemplate the
building of a new and different world.*

We Come to the River

'Actions for Music in Two Parts and Eleven Scenes',
 with music by Hans Werner Henze.
Written: Autumn 1972-Oct. 1974.
First London production: Royal Opera House, Covent
 Garden, 12 July 1976 (dir. Hans Werner Henze; des.
 Jürgen Henze; conductor David Atherton).
Revived: Deutsche Oper, Berlin, 18 Sept. 1976 (dir.
 Volker Schlöndorff); Oper der Stadt, Cologne,
 30 May 1977 (dir. Michael Hampe).
Published: London: Methuen (with *The Fool*), 1976;
 Mainz: B. Schott's Söhne, 1976.

*A General, having been victorious in a bitter campaign, is
told by his doctor that he will shortly lose his sight. He
begins to look with new sympathy on the sufferings of
the war's victims, and, when he renounces publicly the
violence of the society he has served, he is confined in a
madhouse. He gives no encouragement to a soldier who
urges him to lead a revolt of the oppressed people, and
he refuses his Emperor's request for the support that as a
popular hero he could give to a régime faced with civil
war. The soldier assassinates the Governor of the province
and the Emperor has the General blinded. Even the mad
people cannot accept the General's perception of truth;
they 'drown' him beneath the imaginary river that is to
lead them to freedom. The dead victims who had re-
appeared when the General was blinded sing of their
hope in a better future.*

Royal Opera House programme, 12 July 1976

Henze and Bond together have fashioned an event for
the theatre which strips away the accretions of nineteenth-
century practice and presents a simple and avowedly
political message by combining the simplest forms of
acting and music, both vocal and instrumental, on equal
terms. . . . There is no orchestra pit and no orchestra in
the conventional sense. . . . The enlarged stage is divided
into three 'action areas', one on the covered pit, the

second just beyond the proscenium arch, and the third further upstage. Each area has its own instrumental group, seated in formal evening dress. . . . The stage area is defined by three plain wooden walls, supporting a battery of percussion instruments and acting as an acoustic reflector. The period and environment of the action are indicated by costumes and a very few props.

Christopher Hunt, *Opera,* July 1976

I found that when I wrote the libretto for the opera . . . I was not merely providing language to be set to music, in the way a nineteenth-century libretto would be set, but that I was throwing language into a cauldron; that its meaning would have to be recreated by the music; that the music would not merely colour it or comment on it. What had to be done was more radical. It is, of course, only what has to be done whenever anyone now writes a play; a story can no longer teach its own interpretation, and so instead of the story providing the meaning, the dramatist must provide a meaning to the story − that is, he doesn't so much dramatize the story as the interpretation or analysis of it. The sound world Henze created on the text was not a mere montage − though there were many things in it that would have normally passed for pastiche − but an analysis of the various events (which were played on three stages simultaneously).

Bond, quoted in *Companion,* p.23

Orpheus

'A Story in Six Scenes', with music by Hans Werner Henze.
Written: Dec. 1977-Feb. 1978.
First production: Stuttgart Ballet Co., 17 Mar. 1979
    (choreography by William Forsythe), trans, Metropolitan
    Opera House, New York, 25 June 1979.
Unpublished.

A stunning theatre piece impelled by Forsythe's brave response to Henze's highly imaginative score. Bond's scenario and his set of nine Canzoni *to Orpheus which are a commentary on the theme, invert and revise the Orpheus legend, turning the musician/poet into a revolutionary figure who rejects Apollonian inspiration, breaks the lyre that is his contact with the God, to make 'a new*

music'. . . . Visually, as well as dramatically, the piece is concerned
with the harsh poetry to be made from the materials of today.
. . . For Henze, Bond, and Forsythe, the key to Orpheus *is the*
creative artist who breaks entirely with past myth and past
attitudes to force a new world by braving the gods. . . . Its superb-
ly effective setting, by Axel Manthey, is a white boxed set, having
three doors at the side, and at the back a cellar-like entry into
hell, while above this is a neon-lit white corridor with sliding
doors, down which Apollo makes his appearances in clouds of
dry ice.

Clement Crisp, *Financial Times,* 20 Mar. 1979

The Cat

'A Story for Music' in two parts and ten scenes, with music by
   Hans Werner Henze.
Written: Mar.-May 1979.
First production, under the title, *The English Cat:* Schwetzinger
   Festspiele, Württembergische Staatsoper Stuttgart, Schloss
   Schwetzingen, 2 June 1983 (dir. Hans Werner Henze; des.
   Jakob Niedermeier; conducted by Dennis Russell Davies).
Published: London: Methuen, 1982, with *Restoration;* Mainz:
   B. Schott's Söhne, 1983.

Set in London about 1900. All of the figures are animals. Lord
Puff, an aristocratic cat of advancing years, must marry to get an
heir. His nephew, the dissolute Arnold, wishes to prevent the
marriage in order to inherit Puff's wealth. Puff is surrounded by
members of the Royal Society for the Protection of Rats. Puff's
intended bride is Minette, a country cat, who brings her sister,
Babette, to town with her. Minette falls in love with Tom, who
attempts unsuccessfully to prevent the marriage. Minette is accused
of assorted crimes by Puff and Tom defends her at the trial, when
Tom is revealed as the long lost son of Lord Fairport. He must
claim his inheritance before he reaches 21, which is the following
day. Minette, by order of her mistress, is drowned, and Tom is
murdered before he may claim his inheritance. With the RSPR
triumphant, the last word is with the society's tame mouse,
Louise, who revolts, steals the collecting box belonging to the
society, and promises mayhem.

Having said . . . that, in the kind of theatrical form he envisaged
for the future, 'characters wouldn't be moved by personal motives
but by the forces of history. They'd be epic in analysis but not
necessarily in size − after all a mouse can be the hero of an epic',
Bond created his libretto in the form of a beast fable. . . . Its
setting . . . is neither winsome nor sentimental, for its frame of
reference is so clearly to human affairs. In epic terms, it is a story
and an analysis. The analysis is contained within the songs, all of
which speak directly or by implication to the cause of the narrative.
In the first draft, dated April 1979, Bond asked himself: 'What's
in this libretto for me? I must find a new and comprehensive
lyricism, which enables me to deal with simple human experience,
but isn't a re-creation of an already hackneyed past . . .'.

Philip Roberts, 'The Search for Epic Drama:
Edward Bond's Recent Work', Modern Drama, XXIV, 4
(Dec. 1981)

'Everything', Henze wrote to Bond, . . . 'seems sweet and charm-
ing, but then suddenly becomes grim and terrible'. Bond shares
Henze's political sympathies, but he threw in a word of caution:
'I am sure you think as I do . . . but one point I would like to
emphasize. What we don't want is the sort of approach in which
the characters take off their masks and address the public directly
. . . as though we wanted to say, "You have had your fun; now sit
still and listen to our sermon".' *The English Cat* is thus more than
another of Henze's essays in politicized music theatre. It makes
its point tellingly, but it does so without mounting the pulpit.

P. Heyworth, The Observer, 12 June 1983

A Chaste Maid in Cheapside

Adapted from the play by Thomas Middleton (1611).
Written: Nov. 1965.
First London production: Royal Court Th., 13 Jan.
1966 (dir. William Gaskill; des. John Gunter).
Unpublished.

I did a version of *Chaste Maid* for Bill Gaskill, mostly
providing versions for obscure lines with the idea that he
could use any he thought essential, but he wasn't to alter
everything; and also, I rearranged the end. This new
ending was used . . . .
　　　Edward Bond, letter to Philip Roberts, 21 May 1976

A Chaste Maid in Cheapside creaks a good deal, especially
in the first act, as the five grotesque family groups gradually enmesh into the machinery. But the best way to
enjoy it is to sit back, as at music hall, and let the
humour come to you. Between the laughs, it is clear this
is a serious and misanthropic work — rather like a
clownish and caricatured version of *Saved* — with some
quite eerie and surrealist inventions such as the two
pantomime, puritan informers who go sniffing and lip-
smacking in search of citizens smuggling meat in Lent.
　　　Alan Brien, *Sunday Telegraph,* 16 Jan. 1966

Three Sisters

Translation of the play by Anton Chekhov (1901),
　　'assisted from the original Russian' by Richard
　　Cottrell.
Written: Autumn 1966.
First London production: Royal Court Th., 18 Apr.
　　1967 (dir. William Gaskill; des. Abd' Elkader Farrah).
Revived: Northcott Th., Exeter, 29 Sept. 1971 (dir.
　　Jane Howell); Nottingham Playhouse, 24 Oct. 1973
　　(dir. Richard Eyre).
Published: in programme of first production at Royal
　　Court Th.

The translation by Bond is excellent; the best I've ever read or
heard . . . .

Charles Marowitz, *Village Voice*, Apr. 1967
(full review reprinted in his *Confessions of a Counterfeit
Critic* (London: Methuen, 1973), p.126-9

Spring Awakening

Translation of the play by Frank Wedekind (1891).
Written: early 1974.
First London production: National Th., 28 May 1974 (dir.
   Bill Bryden; des. Geoffrey Scott).
Revived: Market Place Th., Vancouver, July 1975 (dir. Dennis
   Eberts).
Published: London: Methuen, 1980, with introduction by
   Elisabeth Bond and Edward Bond.

I should say that Mr. Bond had been scrupulously faithful both
to Wedekind's irony and his poetry.

Charles Lewsen, *The Times*, 29 May 1974

The White Devil

'Acting Edition' of the play by John Webster (1611).
Written: May 1976.
First London production: Old Vic Th., 12 July 1976 (dir.
   Michael Lindsay-Hogg; des. John Gunter; with Glenda Jackson
   as Vittoria, Jack Shepherd as Flamineo, Jonathan Price as
   Lodovico, and Patrick Magee as Monticelso).
Unpublished.

Although Bond's acting version adds almost nothing and makes
very few omissions, the entire production is surely under his spell.
Where Webster's characters are heartless, they remain overtly
frenzied, yet here the inside is turned out to illuminate more
precisely, in a modern context, how passionless our own violence
has become. Where the production does not succeed is in failing
to allow the irrational to subvert its basic coolness. Moments of
severe alarm on the heartless landscape would clarify the major
purpose of the action and provide the strength needed to make

the interpretation whole and workable. Nonetheless, it is in the worthiest spirit of adaptation, surely the season's most misunderstood work.

David Zane Mairowitz, *Plays and Players,* Sept. 1976

a: Stories

The King with Golden Eyes: in *The Pope's Wedding*
(London: Methuen, 1971).

Mr. Dog: in *Gambit*, No.17 (1970).

Christ Wanders and Waits (part of *Sharpeville Sequence*):
in *Gambit*, No.17 (1970), and in *The Pope's Wedding*
(London: Methuen, 1971).

Service: in *Fireweed* No. 3 (1975); in *New Writing and
Writers*, 14 (London: Calder, 1977); and in *Summer*
(London: Methuen, 1982). Read by David Ryall,
BBC Radio 3, 8 Apr. 1983.

*A Story, In Praise of Bad Times, Another Story, Black
Animal, Free Man:* in *The Woman* (London:
Methuen, 1979).

The Team and *A Story:* in *The Activists Papers*, published
with *The Worlds* (London: Methuen, 1980).

*The Dragon, The Boy who threw Bread on the Water,
The Boy who Tried to Reform the Thief, The Good
Traveller, The Cheat, The Fly, The Tree, A Dream,
The Rotten Apple Tree, The Call, On the Pride of
Some who Rule, The Cliffs, A Man Sat on a Gate,
The Wise Man who Broke his Vow, Water, There was
a Cunning, Wealthy Man, Incident on the Island of
Aigge, The Letter:* in *Summer* (London: Methuen,
1982). *Water* and *The Rotten Apple Tree* read by
David Ryall, BBC Radio 3, 25 Mar. and 27 Apr. 1983.

The Girl who Gave away her Sweets and *The Good
Traveller:* in *New Writing and Writers*, 19 (London:
Calder, 1981), with *The Dragon, The Boy who threw
Bread on the Water, The Boy who Tried to Reform
the Thief, The Cheat* and *The Fly.*

b: Poems

Poems written with specific reference to the plays are
noted in Section 2. A selection of poems is available in
Edward Bond: Theatre Poems and Songs, selected and
edited by Malcolm Hay and Philip Roberts (London:
Methuen, 1978). See also poems in *The Activists Papers*,
published with *The Worlds* (London: Methuen, 1980).

c: Screenplays

Bond participated in the middle and late 'sixties in the writing of
a number of film scripts, including *Blow-up, Michael Kolhaas,
Laughter in the Dark, Walkabout,* and *Nicholas and Alexandra.*
On this work he commented in 1971 and 1974:

I write films in order to live. I've never worked on a film script
that interested me deeply — or, if it did, imagined for one moment
that one could be allowed to deal with the subject properly. That's
why all my serious writing is done for the theatre and it's never
interfered with there. . . . Don't waste reader's time by making
them read about this nonsense. It's boring because the subject's
boring. You can't honestly pick out my contributions to the
films, they are so adulterated.

Bond, letters to Richard Scharine, quoted in Scharine,
The Plays of Edward Bond (Lewisburg: Bucknell
UP, 1976), p.159

It seems to me that in modern theatre everything is up for reinterpretation.

Dec. 1982

The Two 'Series' of Early Plays

When I first started seriously to write plays I thought my life's work would be the span of plays that began with *The Pope's Wedding* and in fact ended with *The Sea*. But when I'd finished these plays I found, of course, that there were many other plays I wanted to write. I next wrote three plays (*Bingo*, *The Fool*, and *The Woman*) in which I tried to deal with society at three important stages of cultural development. The past often works as a myth on the present. It is like a burden on our back and from time to time we have to rearrange it so that it becomes comfortable and we can go on with our journey. Writers ought to spend some time dealing with the great ages of the past so that we don't fall into the error of believing in a golden age when all the answers were known — and believing that if we could recreate the social conditions of that age we could possess these answers.

Letter to Tony Coult, 28 July 1977,
quoted in *Companion*, p.74-5

Lines of Development to 'Narrow Road'

...I think you've followed the development of the themes through the plays very well. Scopey, Len, Arthur are of course the same person in different stages of development. Scopey commits the crime, Len witnesses it ambivalently, Arthur is legally involved in the court that tries Len. The Len who appears in *Early Morning* is of course the Len from *Saved*, and the trial in the first act of *Early Morning* is in fact a trial of the whole play *Saved*, seen from Arthur's point of view, which is morally and emotionally more developed than it was when he was called Len (in *Saved*)! So I meant this scene to be a deliberate looking back at the earlier play.

Len-*Early Morning* stresses the identity between himself and Len-Arthur by kicking the dead man's clothes over Len-Arthur — trying to 'clothe' him in the murder scene off-stage — and also pointing out that most of my aggressors are also victims. So that it's appropriate they should wear the dead man's clothes (Len-Arthur and Scopey) and that, in one way, Len-*Saved* plays with the chair like a child with a toy.

The identity between the victim and the aggressor is seen most clearly in Scopey and Kiro. The dualities between the characters are important. The hero always appears with an opposite — Scopey/Alen, Len/Fred, the Twins, Kiro/Shogo — and a lot of the drama comes out of the conflict between these pairs of characters. They are all attracted and repelled by one another — and they all involve the other in death. The development of the plays can be seen most clearly in the developing situation between these pairs. Who is bait and who is victim?

I think the only omission I noticed in your analysis concerns Shogo. You didn't point out that he was the child Basho had abandoned in the Introduction. This again makes Shogo a victim as well as an aggressor, and I wanted to make this point very clear: destruction must always accelerate under the influence of human passions (well, almost always. Some societies have had built-in restraints so that their vendettas [don't] get out of hand). But for us it is true, and the harvest of hate is reaped tenfold. So Shogo, who was killed (emotionally — it comes to the same thing) as a child, later kills five or ten or whatever number it is. Basho is directly responsible for their deaths. He is the villain of the play.

On the question of death and emotions. The pro-life half of the pairs (Scopey, Len, Arthur, Kiro) has been killed off like the others (Alen, Harry, Basho, and others) but not completely killed. In *Pope's Wedding* and *Saved* their state of still being alive is shown by restless curiosity — this may seem a minor thing, but it amounts to the search for truth, and in the contexts in which they find themselves it's miraculous! But in *Early Morning* this becomes more active resistance: Albert won't be dead, literally won't lie still in his coffin — he steals his sword back when their eyes are closed, and can't be quiet as a ghost because Arthur (that part of him which is still alive) keeps him awake; and of course, above all Arthur! Because he finally escapes back to life!

Letter to Irene, 7 Jan. 1970, quoted in *Companion*, p.43-4

Recording Experience in the Early Plays

. . . What happened, you see, is when I started to write I simply recorded, very much recorded, my experience. You've got to remember that before my first play was produced, which was *The Pope's Wedding*, and after that, *Saved*, before they were produced I'd written about fifteen plays and they were all, so far as I remember, or the significant ones in them, simply describing the world I'd grown up in or was living in, and I had this idea that if I described it clearly and accurately, then people would say, 'Well, these things are terrible and we must do something about it'.

Well, when I did produce my first play they didn't say that at all. They said, 'How disgraceful, how dare you put these things on the stage. How dare you show us these things? We don't want to know about that', and I'd rather sort of assumed that there were enough people in society – if you could actually tell them what's going on – [who] would do something about it, [but] no, you got into this whole series of excuses like 'It's their fault', or 'They were born like that', or 'There is nothing we can do about it except punish them for being like that', and things like that. So then it became necessary for me to understand the situation more and to see why things went wrong and what caused them to go wrong and therefore the way you put them into being, make them go right. And my plays since then have been an exploration of the problems of being a human being in the twentieth century and to try to find out why things go wrong and how we could correct them.

The plays have been a process of analysis. The development of the plays is therefore very important; it doesn't mean to say I have to disown my early plays because I didn't, in any of them, write anything which was – which I would disagree with – but if you look at my earlier plays then you won't see any answers, you won't see any solutions, but I hope you will find problems presented truthfully and very powerfully – or as powerfully as I could do it anyway – but you won't find any solutions. You will find that the possibilities of solutions are there; I never write a play in which I am pessimistic or fatalistic, even in a play like *Saved* where the people feel themselves to be very much trapped. At the end I don't let them finish in despair. They are still fighting, still resisting.

So what you have to get from those plays is, I think, a feeling of human strength and resourcefulness and the sense that ordinary people are strong enough to change their situation. That you should be able to get from the early plays, but you won't get any analysis beyond that. You will get a description of the problem and a portrayal of the strength of human beings . . . but the earlier plays have no more than that.

And then, you see, having written *The Pope's Wedding* and *Saved,* my next play, *Early Morning,* is a totally different type

65

of play. People sometimes regard it as surrealistic. I actually don't. I see it as dealing with exactly the same problems as *Saved.* . . . But if *Saved* was a camera set up in a room or a street, *Early Morning* was a camera set up in the head and then, you see, what you find in the head is the total chaos, the politico-psychology of the individuals in *Saved,* and they're living in a nightmare world with its own particular theology of madness, if you like, but which isn't really descriptive of cause and effect in the real world. But even in that chaos I tried to find out that principle by which the leading character can pass a moral judgement on the people that are surrounding him. In other words he can make some moral assessment that he would know Hitler for what Hitler was and that he would know Hitler's victims for what they were.

But it is only a moral, I think, judgement, and therefore, inadequate. It's not a practical political judgement because I didn't have the tools, the understanding. I didn't have the analysis then to make those problems clear in political terms, and the hero of *Early Morning* solves his problems in a sort of abstract, psychological way, and that, I think, is not a full description of what human behaviour should be. It's not a false description but it's an inadequate description and it uses imagery that I wouldn't use now.

Unpublished interview with Salvatore Maiorana, Feb. 1981

Inside and Outside the Prison
Why *Lear*? Partly because of the moral imbalance . . . if you look at these three girls, you'll find they all suffer as much and die like Lear, and are no more guilty than him — that in fact they are like the three sisters [of Chekhov's]. . . . Anyway, unlike *Early Morning* it isn't basically a comedy. The intention is more serious. *Early Morning* was like someone escaping from a prison. Tunnelling their way out. In the new play, they are outside and take a look around. . . .

Note on *Lear,* 1 Dec. 1969

Finding the Right Image
I don't yet have the starting-image. *Early Morning* was the twins, *Narrow Road* was the Basho-baby scene. . . . My own version of *Lear* and the *Three Sisters* isn't enough. I must start from my own image, and not merely my own ideas. . . . I must get my image from the world that isn't on the stage. The park [in *Saved*]

and the Siamese twins are real images, not theatrical ones.
Note on *Lear,* 1 Dec. 1969

There's a certain sort of struggle in people about various parts of themselves, some of which as one gets older one has to get rid of. And if one can't get unity between these various personalities, then one can't achieve coherent action. . . . It's very important for Lear too that he should get rid of this other figure: he has to disown something of himself, this instinctive thing he calls the Gravedigger's Boy. That, incidentally, was the image from which the play grew. . . .

Theatre Quarterly, No.5 (1972)

The End of the First 'Series'
I had to write *Lear* before I wrote *The Sea.* One has to have a whole vision of life. One has to admit the dark things, the hopeless things, the destructive things, but one shouldn't lose one's balance. So if one's going to write a play like *Lear,* in order to give oneself the courage to write that, one must also have in one's mind, 'Yes, but there's also *The Sea*'. I've always used comedy in my plays because it's part of one's rapport with the audience. . . . But the balance is different this time in that I deliberately set out to make an audience laugh. . . . I wanted deliberately to say to the audience: 'You mustn't despair. You mustn't be afraid. You must be conscious of the dangers but nevertheless be conscious of your strengths. Be conscious of your intelligence.'

The Times, 22 May 1973

I wanted to end the series of plays with two people sitting on a beach after the storm has died down, talking to an old man. They try to come to terms with the problems that they have to face. . . . In the first play, the young man kills the old man because there's absolutely no possibility of any communication between them. Not just words, not even feelings. If you cannot convey feelings, then you're really isolated, aren't you? If you're isolated, you become violent, like people in a madhouse. And this leads to murder. In *The Sea,* near the close, someone does come to murder the old man with a stick. But the old man talks sense to him, to this rough, loutish boy. And then the other boy comes

67

on, the educated one. They're both parts of the same character, in a way.

Performing Arts Journal, No.2 (Fall 1976)

I did write [*The Sea*] soon after *Lear* as a sort of commentary on the first play, and there are echoes of Lear in Evens.

Letter to Nick Hern, 1 Feb. 1978

From Problem Plays to Answer Plays

A rational, free culture is based either on a classless society or at least on the conscious struggle to remove class structures and the economic, ecological, psychological, and political distortions they cause. A writer's work should be part of this struggle. I've always felt that, but now I see more clearly what is involved. Of course writing the right sort of plays isn't easy. In *Bingo* I made Shakespeare lament that when he was old he no longer even understood the questions. We mustn't write only problem plays, we must write answer plays – or at least plays which make answers clearer and more practical. When I wrote my first plays, I was, naturally, conscious of the weight of the problems. Now I've become more conscious of the strength of human beings to provide answers. The answers aren't always light, easy, or even straightforward, but the purpose – a socialist society – is clear.

Letter to Tony Coult, 28 July 1977, quoted in
Companion, p.75

From Bond's Notebook for 'Bingo'

Notes for a chamber drama.

WS living at New Place and dying there. Last part of his life.

Jonson and Drayton drink with WS at an inn. Earlier that day WS is at a public execution or punishment. Victim, a poor man. WS gets drunk. Goes home. Stops outside the house, in the snow. Talks. Susanna comes to get him. He won't go in – the dark house. Wife(?) and Judith come and help her to carry, support WS into house. Could end here, or last scene in his bedroom.

WS not writing at this time. . . .

The history of the enclosure isn't followed through and isn't the main subject. It is how it makes WS act that concerns the play. . . .

The scenes to be short, dry, and factual, especially at the beginning.

Set: the hard factual world of commerce; the logical contriving and arranging; constructing, and detailed defining of consequences; the legitimate search for security.

Against: human doubt and vulnerability; the inescapable biological cage (which is made more of damp rope than solid iron, but can't be got completely away from).

Consider: how do the two relate? How personal security can lead to selfishness, and moral justification of unfairness. WS would say none of these things, but they would be presented to him.

So WS must die unsatisfied and unhappy. . . .

No effort to show WS at work or as a writer, or how the great man eats an egg etc. . . .

What is WS doing at New Place? Has he come back to make money, play the local gentleman, ignore or forget his literary experience? Can't be. Whether very consciously or not, [it] will have made him what he now is. He may appear to be a local gentleman, but he is the author of the world's greatest plays. They were not written in a dream, and his hands were not the unconscious agents for the experience of what it is like being human. He has been to Golgotha and the clay will always cling to his boots. So he has come back to *be* WS dying and not a local gentleman making money. . . .

Preliminary notes for *Bingo,* 2 and 10 Apr. 1973

Building a Production: to a Director of 'The Fool'

Scene One. The approach described in your letter is right. The 'Mummers'' play shouldn't be gauche — like the rustics' play in *Midsummer Night's Dream.* We should feel they have their own expertise, that their clothes have a real eye for colour and design — they aren't at all Walt Disneyish. They should be very competent dancers and singers: it is their culture, and they can still express themselves in it. They can, of course, poke fun at Milton and the Parson, but they still have to show their respect: it has to be suggested, not stated aggressively. Darkie's Napoleon dress — a hat perhaps — is good. Patty would join in the dancing and singing — because by then the atmosphere would have heightened. Introducing the Parson's speech shouldn't be difficult: he's a parson and he gives sermons, always and everywhere. It's as simple as that. They've had their bit of fun, now he will give the lesson. There is also an ulterior motive: he's probably consciously preparing the parish for the changes Milton's going to make. The Parson has probably been buttering them up for some time now

— they almost expect hints (I mean the farm labourers). But they don't really understand it, it hasn't been spelt out in so far as it affects them: Clare is still surprised, and Patty and Darkie are still shocked and frightened, in Scene Two. (Patty's also very frightened about Darkie's violence to one of Milton's men, in Scene Two: it's like being identified as a Jew in Nazi Germany, Milton knows how to destroy troublemakers.) 'Gon all hot when he look at me' refers to Milton. She's embarrassed and fancies that he fancies her: Milton probably had some reputation when he was a young man, probably unfounded (though not necessarily so).

Young girls of her class would have always been conscious of the sexual element in their relationships with the upper classes, even if the element was only potential: after all, it was the one time in their lives when they had something to offer that was needed. Patty probably feels herself to be, in an almost literal way, perishable goods. It makes her suggestion to Clare, in Scene Two, that he can go off with Mary, if he likes, quite courageous — even is the risk is slight, and she'd promptly withdraw the offer if Clare seemed like suggesting it, still he *could* use it against her and so she's taken a risk with her whole life, not just marriage, but work, comfort, food. [The letter continues with a similarly detailed analysis of the later scenes.]

From a letter to Louis Scheeder, on his production
for the Folger Th. Group, Washington, Nov. 1976

Early Thoughts on 'Restoration'
The following are extracts taken from Edward Bond's notebooks between Nov. 1979 and July 1980, and were written before the first draft of the play.

To tell a story. The actor should not try to experience what it is like to be a character. He should take pleasure in telling the story. He is first of all — above all — himself. As a storyteller he imitates the character about which he is telling — from time to time he imitates him almost rudely, almost with a wink, as if to say: this is the guy exactly.

To avoid nihilism drama has to accept that man not only acts but is acted upon by non-human forces, such as technology and the natural scene — and that his 'self' is concerned more with the social relationships by which the group tackles its economic and natural relationships. So psychology is social and political. . . . To act a life, not a character. To show people in relation to their determinants. This is not a passive relationship . . . man's moral responsibility must be shown not to be to himself — to save his soul — but to his community.

People do things as a result of their beliefs and opinions. Very often what they believe and think is decided not by rational thought but by the unconscious motivations of their class position. People tend to see the world from their own view of it. These things can make up much of the texture of a play — the grain in the wood. . .

To laugh at the fools in power. To laugh at the weak fools who have power within their grasp but won't take it. . . . But do I need to deal with laughter *in* the play, as a political force, as a weapon?

Lord Are's attitude to life is quite mechanical. He's like a machine processing life so that he will remain 'on top'. At the same time he admires himself and is vain. What does he enjoy?

There should be wit in Bob's insistence on seeing Lord Are in a good light and (when that's no longer possible) then the institutions Lord Are represents. But how can this be done without making Bob contemptible? What would Rose see in him? . . . Mustn't be a . . . milksop. . . . That men put their neck in the noose is known. It is not always understood that they also build the gallows and pay the hangman.

Themes: (i) the appearance of freedom without the reality; (ii) the manipulation of working class consciousness; (iii) Rose's London 'experiences' as a grounding for protest and action. She isn't immediately, naturally free — she has to win her own freedom in the play — and then try to help Bob to win his. . .

I find that my work is more radical than I had thought. I began writing simply as a criticism of certain things I saw around me, and in praise of certain other things. I wanted to understand and so I had to analyze. I didn't at that time understand the implications this would have on my theatrical technique.

What [the actor] has to act are the situations. The situations are designed [to] show what *forms* the character. He shows us not a character acting but a character being formed . . . in interaction with his world. . . . I am often called a moralist. But I am a moralist only in a special sense. First I am a politician. I see politics as an expression of morality. . . . To reach Utopia, you do not behave as if you were already in it. . .

At the moment it seems as if I'm writing a satire, an opera of death. I am not — a comedy must affirm not merely the values by which it criticizes; it must reach beyond the stage and show the practices by which those values will be established in actual life. A comedy must not merely be a morality, it must be a political play.

Instead of becoming Satanic, Lord Are could become smaller, fussier ... that he almost would murder someone to go to a *soirée* ...

Ibsen, probing deeper than the boulevardier dramatists, used gremlins and trolls to substantiate reality: these are mysterious entities beyond human analysis and control. The intervention of the outside entities is what made human life difficult to understand or control. Dramatists now have to find how to dramatize reality — the meaning of the appearance of things — in such a way that it can be understood, and that the means of controlling it may also be understood ...

I feel the killing [of Ann] should be an act of great theatrical brilliance. Why? Why not a sordid little scuffle? From whose point of view? That is the chief dramatic question: from whose point of view?

I am now able to start the play of *Restoration* because the characters have enough texture for me and because the gesture of the play is clear to me.

The Genesis of 'Summer'
These further extracts from Edward Bond's notebooks were written between August and October 1980, again before the first draft of the play.

Is it a pattern play (such as the second half of *The Woman*) where events are plotted so as to be a diagram of history, where the characters represent forces; or is it an examination of a *real* event, where the historical forces can be seen, as in a shop window — or as in a glance through a window into a living room? It ought to be the second if I can make it so. I would like to show how the daily is involved in the politically universal and that it is reflected in character but not in specific acts ...

A possible method. Let the first section be normal. About daily things and daily complexities involving the holidaying [Xenia], the dying Marthe and the young couple. Then go to the Island so that the first section meets its counterpart, its illumination —

involving the visit of the [German, as Xenia's] shadow. Then a final section which joins the two and draws the lesson and in which Marthe dies. . . . I want a process that will reveal a process.

The worlds of *Summer*. The worlds of the daily activity — preparing food, eating, cleaning. . . . The world of discussion — that is, the reflective ideas that make sense of the lives that the characters have led. . . . The world of the drama, Xenia against Marthe . . .

Enlarge sense of play as much as possible. Xenia has had her social being removed: property, citizenship, customary relations etc. — everything except her life and what culture . . . she takes with her. Marthe also begins a new life. The old relations, strengthened by accepted customs, attitudes, and ways, are gone. The old society, with its economic and industrial hardware and super-structures, is gone . . .

The connection between Xenia and [the German] must be made in a pure and simple way. It must be clear — it needs telling only in the sense of showing. . . . The difficulty is that it doesn't involve a connection between individuals (in this play) but between classes; and it's meant to penetrate Xenia's cultural disguise, because she believes she stands for everything that [the German] is against. . . . It's like connecting two people who stand on mountain tops far distant from each other. . . . Perhaps I need steps, stages. If Xenia denies that the Nazis had any respect for her, [the German] says he can prove it. . . . They let a hostage go because you commanded it. The idea of the girl in white (innocence) on the balcony (raised in the air like an icon over an altar) is good. . . . It must seem when [the German] describes [Xenia] that he is describing a person very different from Xenia. . . . Xenia as she was during the war. We have to see how she functions for him. . . . Make the difference as marked as possible.

In a socialist play we ought to see the characters not as more abstract than in other plays, but as more human: the evil should be shown in the ripeness of their evil; the good should be able to express themselves fully: but the analysis must be clearer. Human qualities should not be allowed to obscure or mystify social relationships.

It is partly a play of after-action: a dying woman, a reminiscing visitor, an ex-criminal visiting the scene of his crime. But there are also young people contemplating the future. But they must also be active: they are *creating* an understanding, and this must be produced through *action*, not passive contemplation. . . . What

Marthe needs to do is to speak the truth to the Son and Daughter
... to speak the simple truth so that they can learn of her experience and learn of the precision of judging. The great peripeteia in
the play is the turning from the death cell, guarded by monsters,
and preparing to face guns, to the sun-lit balconies, with the meal
laid on the clean table and the loving son.

The Writer as Director

The reason why I want to direct my plays is that they are experimental without being obviously so. . . .The use of language is
often very contrived, very unreal, although the whole thing is
meant to give the appearance of naturalism. So, in order to write
better for actors, I have to become part of their rehearsal process.
If I say I want actors to be of a different sort, I have to get
involved in the actual technique of creating it with the actor. I
can't any longer be in the situation of nudging someone and
getting them to relay the message. It's simpler and more economic
if I do it myself. Once the play has been done, and I've been able
to understand what all the operational problems are, I can then
revise and put instructions in the text.

Unpublished interview with Patricia Curran, 1 July 1979

On Writing

I don't know how to write plays, I don't know how to write
anything. I have some skills that would enable me to 'write well'.
I know of many writers who use their skills to do that ... But
you ought not to use your skills to write well. Use them to
struggle — to understand the conflicts that shape history, the
tensions and compromises which make society possible, and
which are shown equally (one causing the other) in the objective
world and in human subjective experience. The writer is a reporter
at the most important and most tense of battles — and he has to
use his skill to report what he finds there. And reporting that will
smash the structure of the well-made, well-balanced play — and
the skills will not become self-congratulatory in their competence
but will be transformed because they are always under stress.
That means, you never know how to write it but are always
learning how to write it.

Letter to Dick Edwards, 12 June 1982

a: Primary Sources

Collections
cited elsewhere by short titles, as below

Plays: One, with an introduction. London: Methuen, 1977. [*Saved, Early Morning, The Pope's Wedding.*]
Plays: Two, with an introduction. London: Methuen, 1978. [*Lear, The Sea, Narrow Road to the Deep North, Black Mass, Passion.*]
The Activists Papers, in *The Worlds.* London: Methuen, 1980. [An important group of papers on dramatic theory.]

Articles and Essays

Letters to *Guardian,* 12 Sept. 1965; and to *Evening Standard,* 21 and 23 Nov. 1965. [Bond's reaction to hostile criticism of *Saved.*]
'Millstones round the Playwright's Neck', *Plays and Players,* Apr. 1966. [On critics and state censorship of the theatre.]
The Writer's Theatre, issued with the programme of *Lear,* Royal Court Th., 29 Sept. 1971; reprinted in *Companion,* p.44-7. [The importance of the Royal Court for playwrights.]
Reply to Roger Manvell's review of *Lear, Humanist,* Feb. 1972. [Bond's view of his play.]
'Letter to Arthur Arnold', *Theatre Quarterly,* No.6 (Apr.-June 1972). [Disputing Arnold's view of the plays.]
'Beating Barbarism', *Sunday Times,* 25 Nov. 1973. [Reply to Harold Hobson's review of *Bingo.*]
'Exercises for Young Writers', 21 Mar. 1977; reprinted in *Companion,* p.48-50. [Notes on a workshop held at the Royal Court.]
'Work in Hand', *The Guardian,* 13 Jan. 1978. [Bond's account of *The Bundle.*]
'On Brecht: a Letter to Peter Holland', *Theatre Quarterly,* No.30 (1978), p.34-5. [Bond's account of Brecht's influence on him.]
'Us, Our Drama, and the National Theatre', *Plays and Players,* Oct. 1978.

'The Romans and the Establishment's Figleaf', *The Guardian,*
    3 Nov. 1980. [Defence of Howard Brenton's *The Romans in*
    Britain.]
'Reply to David Roper', *Gambit,* No.36 (1980), p.33-4.
    [Criticizing Roper's earlier review of *The Worlds.*]
'The Theatre I Want', in *At The Royal Court,* ed. R. Findlater
    (Ambergate: Amber Lane Press, 1981), p.121-4. [Bond on
    how theatre should develop.]

Interviews

Plays and Players, Nov. 1965, with R. Cushman.
The Guardian, 11 Apr. 1966, with D. Malcolm.
Town, May 1966, with J. Wilson.
Transatlantic Review, XXII (1966), p.7-15, with Giles Gordon;
    reprinted in *Behind the Scenes: Theatre and Film Interviews*
    from the Transatlantic Review, ed. J.F. McCrindle (London:
    Pitman, 1971), p.125-36.
'Thoughts on Contemporary Theatre', *New Theatre Magazine,*
    VII, 2 (Spring 1967), p.6-13. [Edited transcript of a discussion
    between Bond, David Storey, *et. al.,* at Cheltenham Festival of
    Literature.]
Sunday Times, 31 Mar. 1968, with A. Brien.
Evening News, 7 Feb. 1969, with J. Green.
The Observer, 9 Feb. 1969, with R. Bryden.
Harper's Bazaar, Mar. 1969, with S. Beauman.
Peace News, 10 Apr. 1969, with A. Arnold.
Telegraph and Argus, 27 Sept. 1969, with C. Russell.
Vogue, Oct. 1969, with M. Warner.
'A Discussion with Edward Bond', *Gambit,* No.17 (1970), p.5-38.
The Guardian, 29 Sept. 1971, with J. Hall.
New York Times, 2 Jan. 1972, with C. Marowitz.
Theatre Quarterly, No.5 (1972), p.4-14, with the editors.
Times, 22 May 1973, with R. Hayman.
Observer, 11 Aug. 1974, with H. Dawson.
Guardian, 15 Aug. 1974, with H. Hebert.
Chicago Tribune, 17 Nov. 1974, with R. Dettmer.
Sunday Times, 2 Nov. 1975, with P. Oakes.
Plays and Players, Dec. 1975, with T. Coult.
New Haven Register, 25 Jan. 1976, with M. Leech.
Time Out, 11-17 June 1976, with R. Krupp.
Gay News, 17-30 June 1976, with K. Howes.
Observer Magazine, 18 July 1976, with J. Walker.

Performing Arts Journal, I, 2 (1976), p.37-45, with G. Loney.
The Guardian, 24 Nov. 1976, with N. de Jongh.
Twentieth Century Literature, XXII, 4 (Dec. 1976), p.411-22, with K.H. Stoll.
British Council Literature Study Aids, 1978, with P. Roberts.
Time Out, 13-19 Jan. 1978, with T. Coult.
The Observer, 15 Jan. 1978, with V. Radin.
Dartington Theatre Papers, Second Series (1978), with P. Hulton.
Time Out, 11-17 Aug. 1978, with C. Itzin.
Morning Star, 18 Aug. 1978, with C. Chambers.
Gambit, No.36 (1980), p.34-45, with D. Roper.
Scypt Journal, No.6 (Sept. 1980), p.4-10, with T. Coult.
The Guardian, 31 July 1981, with C. Itzin.

b: Secondary Sources

Full-Length Studies

P. Iden, *Edward Bond*. Velber bei Hanover: Friedrich, 1973. [A short book, with some factual errors, of basic information about the plays up to *The Sea*.]

H. Oppel and S. Christenson, *Edward Bond's Lear and Shakespeare's King Lear*. Mainz: Akademie der Wissenschaften und der Literatur, 1974. [Two pieces on *Lear* and *King Lear*, and on the 'common man' in both plays.]

R. Scharine, *The Plays of Edward Bond*. Lewisburg: Bucknell University Press, 1976. [Sympathetic study of the plays up to *The Sea*.]

S. Trussler, *Edward Bond*. Harlow: Longmans, 1976. [Short but detailed study up to *Bingo*.]

T. Coult, *The Plays of Edward Bond*. London: Methuen, second ed., 1979. [Best short study to date.]

M. Hay and P. Roberts, *Bond: a Study of his Plays*. London: Methuen, 1980. [Full-length study using the early drafts to examine the evolution and stage production of the plays.]

Articles and Chapters in Books

B. Levin, *Daily Mail*, 10 Dec. 1962. [Enthusiastic review of Bond's first performed play, *The Pope's Wedding*.]

H. Kretzmer, *Daily Express*, 4 Nov. 1965. [Typifies the hostile critical reception of *Saved*.]

L. Olivier, *The Observer,* 28 Nov. 1965. [Olivier's celebrated letter in defence of *Saved.*]

P. Ansorge, 'Directors in Interview, No.2: Jane Howell', *Plays and Players,* Oct. 1968. [Interview with the director of *Narrow Road* in Coventry and London.]

H. Hobson, *Sunday Times,* 16 Mar. 1969. [A characteristic misreading of *Early Morning.*]

M. Esslin, *Plays and Players,* Apr. 1969. [Careful analysis of *Saved* and *Narrow Road.*]

D.A.N. Jones, 'A Unique Style of Theatre', *Nova,* July 1969. [Bond's early theatrical style.]

I. Wardle, 'Interview with William Gaskill', *Gambit,* No.17 (1970), p.38-43. [Gaskell's productions of Bond's early work at the Royal Court.]

M. Esslin, 'The Theatre of Edward Bond', *Times Educational Supplement,* 24 Sept. 1971. [Analysis of Bond's work up to *Lear.*]

'Interview with Harry Andrews', *Plays and Players,* Nov. 1971. [The actor who played Lear in London.]

I. Wardle, 'The British Sixties', *Performance,* I, 1 (Dec. 1971), p.174-81. [On Bond's vision of society.]

J.R. Taylor, *The Second Wave.* London: Methuen, 1971, p.77-93. [Development of the plays up to *Passion.*]

G. Dark, 'Production Casebook, No.5: Edward Bond's *Lear* at the Royal Court', *Theatre Quarterly,* No.5 (1972), p.20-31. [Rehearsal logbook by the play's assistant director.]

A. Arnold, 'Lines of Development in Bond's Plays', *Theatre Quarterly,* No.5 (1972), p.15-19.

K. Worth, *Revolutions in Modern English Drama.* London: Bell, 1972, p.168-87. [Careful appraisal of the plays up to *Lear.*]

E. King, 'Violence Defended', *New Haven Register,* Apr. 1973. [Interview with David Giles, director of *Lear* at Yale.]

G. Gow, 'Putting on the Style', *Plays and Players,* Aug. 1973. [Interview with Deirdre Clancy, designer of *The Sea* at the Royal Court.]

P. Ansorge, 'Glittering in the Gorbals', *Plays and Players,* Apr. 1974. [Comments by Philip Prowse on his designs for *Saved* at Citizens' Th., Glasgow.]

Interview with Arthur Lowe, *The Times,* 10 Aug. 1974. [Actor who played Jonson in London *Bingo.*]

P. Gems, letter to *Plays and Players,* Nov. 1974. [Powerful defence of *Bingo.*]

A. Hunt, 'A Writers' Theatre', *New Society,* 11 Dec. 1975. [Claims that Bond's preoccupation with 'a writers' theatre' is self-indulgent.]

J. Worthen, 'Endings and Beginnings: Edward Bond and the Shock of Recognition', *Educational Theatre Journal,* XXVII, 4 (1975), p.466-79. [One of the best accounts of the positive nature of Bond's work.]

N. Yuasa (transl. and ed.), *The Narrow Road to the Deep North and Other Travel Sketches.* Harmondsworth: Penguin, 1966, reprinted 1975. The source book for *Narrow Road.*

T. Browne, *Playwrights' Theatre: The English Stage Company at the Royal Court,* London: Pitman, 1975. A very useful, short account of the company, with numerous references to Bond.

J. Lahr, *Plays and Players,* Jan. 1976. [Acute review of *The Fool.*]

Theatre Quarterly, No. 21 (1976). [Includes W. Donohue, 'Production Casebook, No.21: Edward Bond's *The Fool* at the Royal Court Theatre'; P. Gill, 'Coming Fresh to *The Fool*' (an interview with the director); Edward Bond, 'An Introduction to *The Fool*'; M. Esslin, 'Nor Yet a "Fool" to Fame' (a survey of the critical reaction to the production).]

M. Coveney, 'Space Odyssey', *Plays and Players,* June 1976. [Interview with John Napier, Hayden Griffin, and William Dudley about the designs for *Lear, Bingo,* and *The Fool.*]

Interview with Hans Werner Henze, *The Times,* 9 July 1976. [On his collaboration with Bond.]

A. Jellicoe, 'Royal Court Theatre Writers' Group', *Ambit,* No.68 (1976), p.61-4. [The formation and work of the group, including Bond's part in it.]

D. Clancy, 'Drawings for *Lear*', *Ambit,* No.68 (1976), p.93-5. [Sketches of *Lear* designs for the Royal Court.]

R. Cohn, *Modern Shakespeare Offshoots.* Princeton University Press, 1976, p.254-66. [*Lear* and *King Lear.*]

M. Hay and P. Roberts, 'Edward Bond: Stages in a Life', *Observer Magazine,* 6 Aug. 1978. [On the first company reading of *The Woman.*]

P. Holland, 'Brecht, Bond, Gaskill, and the Practice of Political Theatre', *Theatre Quarterly,* No.30 (1978), p.24-34.

P. Hulton, 'An Interview with Howard Davies', *Dartington Theatre Papers,* Second Series (1978), p.9-17. [Good discussion with the director of *The Bundle* and other of Bond's plays.]

P. Merchant, 'The Theatre Poems of Bertolt Brecht, Edward Bond, and Howard Brenton', *Theatre Quarterly,* No.34 (1979), p.49-51.

P. Roberts, ' "Making the Two Worlds One" – the Plays of Edward Bond', *Critical Quarterly,* XXI, 4 (1979), p.80-8.

[Analysis up to *The Worlds.*]

C. Itzin, *Stages in the Revolution.* London: Methuen, 1980.
[Study of British political theatre since 1968 with a good
section on Bond.]

J. Bryce, 'Rehearsing Optimism', *The Leveller,* No.60 (10-24 July
1981). [Rehearsals for *The Worlds* and *Restoration.*]

P. Roberts, 'The Search for Epic Drama: Edward Bond's Recent
Work', *Modern Drama,* XXIV, 4 (1981), p.458-78. [The
developing dramatic theory, with reference to *Orpheus, The
Worlds, The Cat, Restoration* and *Summer.*]

K. Worth, 'Bond's *Restoration*', *Modern Drama,* XXIV, 4 (1981),
p.479-93. [Close account of the play and its London
production.]

Interview with Yvonne Bryceland, *The Times,* 23 Jan. 1982.
[Actress who played Marthe in *Summer.*]

J. Fenton, *Sunday Times,* 31 Jan. 1982. [Attack on Bond's
politics as demonstrated in *Summer.*]

Interview with Bob Peck, *The Guardian,* 28 June 1982. [Actor
who played Lear at Stratford.]

J. Fenton, *Sunday Times,* 4 July 1982. [The revival of *Lear* at
Stratford and the great quality of the play.]

P. Roberts, 'Edward Bond's *Summer:* "A Voice from the Working
Class" ', *Modern Drama,* XXVI, 2 (1983), p.127-38. [Detailed
analysis of the writing of the play, using Bond's notebooks.]

S. Callow, *Being An Actor.* London: Methuen, 1984. [Callow's
account of working with Bond as a director of *Restoration.*]

T. Eagleton, 'Nature and Violence: the Prefaces of Edward Bond',
Critical Quarterly, XXVI, 1 and 2 (Spring and Summer 1984),
p.127-35. [The range and content of the prefaces.]

Reference Sources

K.-H. Stoll, *The New British Drama.* Bern, Herbert Lang, 1975.
[Bibliography with special reference to Bond, Arden, Osborne,
Pinter, and Wesker.]

K. King, *Twenty Modern British Playwrights: a Bibliography,
1956 to 1976.* New York: Garland, 1977, p. 43-54.

M. Hay and P. Roberts, *Edward Bond: a Companion to the Plays.*
London: TQ Publications, 1978. [Includes detailed
chronology, bibliography, documentation, and fullest listing of
world-wide reviews of the plays.]